Soups & Stews

STOCKS TO ONE-POT MEALS

CYNTHIA SCHEER
Writer and Food Stylist

MICHAEL LAMOTTE
Photographer

COLE
GROUP

Cynthia Scheer is a food writer and home economist. She has been a magazine food editor, and has written 28 cookbooks on a variety of subjects. Other books by Cynthia Scheer from Cole Goup include *Affordable Elegant Meals, Breads, Breakfasts & Brunches,* and *Salads.* A resident of the San Francisco Bay Area, she has traveled extensively throughout the United States, Mexico, and Europe to explore and experience the foods of different regions.

Front Cover

This trio of homemade soups, teamed with your favorite breads and muffins, is hearty enough to be served as a main course. Create your own variations on the basic recipes found in this book by using familiar ingredients you have on hand.

Title Page

Depending on the type of winter squash used, Golden Squash Soup can vary in color from a deep orange to creamy yellow. Finely diced red bell peppers can be sautéed along with the onion for added flavor and color (page 26).

Back Cover

Upper   Flavorful Chicken Corn Soup is just one of the delicious soups that can be prepared using homemade Chinese Chicken Stock (page 66).

Lower   There are as many styles of minestrone soup as there are regions in Italy. Smoked ham hocks and cooked rice combine with other savory ingredients to produce this version from Milan, Minestrone Milanese (page 56).

Special Thanks To   BIA Cordon Bleu; M & M Ferris; Naomi Gonzalez; Janet H. Johnson; Sue Fisher King; Maggie Blyth Klein; Connie Nicholson; Phil Quattrociocchi, S.F. International Cheese Imports; Sebring Sales; Robert Steffy; Sue Williams

Cole books are available for quantity purchases for sales promotions, premiums, fund-raising, or educational use. For more information on Cole's Kitchen Arts Series or other Cole culinary titles, please write or call the publisher.

Contributors

Editor
Karin Shakery

Additional Photographers
Laurie Black; Keith Ovregaard, front cover; Tom Tracy, page 69; Jackson Vereen, page 28

Additional Food Stylists
Susan Massey Weil, page 28; Amy Nathan, pages 4 and 45; Jeff Van Hanswyk

Photographic Stylist
Sara Slavin

Calligrapher
Chuck Wertman

Designers
Linda Hinrichs, Carol Kramer

The Cole's Kitchen Arts Series is published by the staff of Cole Group, Inc.

Publisher
Brete C. Harrison

VP and Director of Operations
Linda Hauck

VP Marketing and Business Development
John A. Morris

VP and Associate Publisher
James Connolly

Senior Editor
Annette Gooch

Editorial Assistant
Lynn Bell

Production Coordinator
Dotti Hydue

© 1995 Cole Group, Inc.

All rights reserved under international and Pan-American copyright conventions.

Printed in Hong Kong through Mandarin Offset.

G F E D C B A
1 0 9 8 7 6 5

ISBN 1-56426-066-6
Library of Congress Catalog Card Number 94-25453

Address all inquiries to
Cole Group, Inc.
1330 N. Dutton Ave., Suite 103
PO Box 4089
Santa Rosa, CA 95402-4089
(800) 959-2717 (707) 526-2682
FAX (707) 526-2687

Distributed to the book trade by
Publishers Group West.

C O N T E N T S

The heart of many of the soups and stews in this book is a flavorsome homemade broth. See pages 8–11 for recipes for making your own.

Soups & Stews for All Seasons

The line that separates a soup from a stew is very fine. It is probably a matter of liquid or, if you will, soupiness. An ill-defined but much-savored middle ground consists of dishes in which meats, poultry, or fish cook in an abundant broth. Such dishes as French *bouillabaisse* and *petite marmite*, Italian *bollito misto*, and Austrian *Tafelspitz* are but a few examples of this sort of one-pot resourcefulness. In short, soups and stews offer a multitude of delicious opportunities— and that is the subject of this cookbook.

Equipment for a soup and stew cook's kitchen includes a stockpot, large kettle, Dutch oven, covered frying pan, and other commonly owned equipment, all described here.

SOUP-MAKING TOOLS

Both soups and stews are such basic kinds of dishes that one hardly needs a sophisticated *batterie de cuisine* to do them justice. But experienced cooks find the following items helpful, and if you enjoy this kind of cooking, it will be useful to accumulate some or all of these utensils.

A *big, heavy stockpot* is essential for making your own broth. When you start with a quantity of bones, they take up a lot of room. The beef broth on page 8, for example, needs a kettle that holds at least 12 quarts; the chicken broth on page 8, an 8- to 10-quart one.

For most of the first-course soups in the second chapter, a *3-quart saucepan* is needed. Remember the rule of thumb that a heavier pan heats more evenly—but it should not be so heavy that it is hard to handle.

For the full-meal soups in the third chapter, a versatile pan is a *5- to 6-quart Dutch oven or deep kettle.*

This will also be useful for many of the traditional stews in this book.

Many family stews, a number of which can be quickly put together on top of the range, make good use of a *deep 10- to 12-inch frying pan with a cover.*

To strain out the bones and vegetables from homemade broth, you need two things: a *large colander* with fine perforations, to fit without spilling or tipping over a *great big bowl* that can withstand the high temperature of the hot broth.

For turning cooked vegetable mixtures into creamy, elegant purées, you will need a *blender or food processor.* Both do the job superbly, but the food processor offers the additional convenience of grating, shredding, slicing, and chopping vegetables and other soup and stew ingredients. You can also use a hand-operated *food mill* to purée vegetables.

SAVING SOUPS AND STEWS FOR A RAINY DAY

The home freezer has revolutionized meal preparation. It provides more free time for the cook, makes advance preparation feasible, and simplifies providing spur-of-the-moment meals for unexpected guests.

Few foods freeze as easily or as well as soups and stews. Following are some convenient ideas for freezing them at different stages.

Bones Pack bones (beef, chicken, or whatever) in sealed, heavy plastic bags or in freezer paper until you are ready to make broth.

Broth Freeze broth in quantities you can use easily to make soups and stews. About 1 quart is a good amount for a first-course soup; measured 1- and 2-cup amounts are useful for stews. Use plastic or coated-cardboard freezer containers, coffee or shortening cans, or glass jars. Remember to leave about an inch of room at the top of the container to allow for expansion of the liquid as it freezes.

Finished Soups These can go into the freezer ready to heat and serve. Mark them with the freezing date, because they should be used within four months. Reheat over direct low heat, stirring often, unless the soup contains milk; creamy soups should be reheated in a double boiler over simmering water.

A soup thickened with egg, such as the Danish Asparagus and Chicken Soup (page 30), may break down on reheating. If you wish to prepare such a soup ahead and freeze it, wait to add the egg until after the frozen soup is thawed and reheated.

Bright, fresh, green vegetables that are added toward the end of cooking in recipes such as Minestrone Milanese (page 56) will be more appealing if you wait to add them until the frozen soup has been reheated and is nearly ready to serve.

Stews Stews are somewhat trickier to freeze than soups. The factor that determines successful freezing is the thickening agent. If the stew is thickened simply by cooking it down until the liquid in it is of a substantial consistency—until it has enough body not to run all over the plate—then the stew can be frozen with no special precautions.

Stew thickened with flour or cornstarch may break down and separate after freezing. If you plan to freeze such a stew to serve later, substitute rice flour, tablespoon for tablespoon for flour or 2 tablespoons to 1 for cornstarch.

Treat egg-thickened stews in the same manner as you would an egg-thickened soup (see above).

If stews contain tender green vegetables, both the color and texture will be much better if you add the vegetables after defrosting and reheating. Use frozen stews within four to six months of storing them.

Freezing raw ingredients for soups and stews allows you to take advantage of specials offered in the supermarket. Heavy-duty foil is ideal for molding tightly around awkwardly shaped whole chickens.

7

STOCK UP ON HOMEMADE BROTH

The mainstay of a sturdy soup (or even a light, delicate one) is a well-made broth. It is not difficult to prepare your own beef, chicken, fish, or vegetable broth. You'll need a large pot, a mélange of flavorful vegetables available the year around, and enough time to let the broth simmer until it becomes a delicious, full-bodied infusion of all that has gone into it. Fortunately, once the broth begins to cook gently, you can leave it alone for hours without attention.

As the broth cooks down, the flavor becomes quite concentrated, so it is best not to add salt until you use the stock. Otherwise you may find that a dish made with the stock has inadvertently become too salty.

Broth is more than the heart of a good soup. On its own, beef or chicken broth that has been clarified (see page 11) stars as sparkling consommé. Broth also makes a delicious liquid ingredient in many stews, sauces, and gravies. And you will treasure your homemade broth as an ingredient for transforming ordinary rice into a perfect pilaf.

HOMEMADE BROTHS

STURDY BEEF BROTH

Thanks to an abundance of bones, this broth is sturdy indeed. It contains so much natural gelatin that as it chills it becomes a quivery solid.

> 8 to 10 pounds meaty beef bones
> 1 veal shank (1 to 1¼ lbs), cut across bone into 2-inch slices
> 3 medium carrots
> 3 large onions
> 2 stalks celery, with leaves, chopped
> 1 can (1 lb) tomatoes
> Salt (optional)

1. Preheat oven to 450° F. Place bones in a large, open roasting pan in a single layer. Top with 1 of the carrots (sliced) and 1 of the onions (thinly sliced). Bake, uncovered, until meat and bones are well browned (about 30 minutes).

2. Transfer the mixture to a large, deep kettle (at least 12-quart size). Add a little water to roasting pan and stir to dissolve brown drippings; add to bone mixture in kettle. Add remaining carrots and onions (chopped), the celery, and the tomatoes (coarsely chopped) with their liquid. Add enough water to cover bones. Bring to a boil, cover, reduce heat, and simmer for 10 to 12 hours.

3. Strain the broth and return it to cooking pot. Boil gently, uncovered, until it is reduced by about a fourth (30 to 45 minutes).

4. Moisten a large piece of muslin or cheesecloth; wring out thoroughly. Line a large colander with several thicknesses of the cloth; place in large bowl. Strain the broth through the cloth. Taste, and add salt if desired. Cover and refrigerate broth for several hours or overnight.

5. Remove fat and discard. Place broth in containers and seal tightly to store. Freeze; or cover and refrigerate, and use within 3 to 4 days.

Makes 10 to 12 cups.

RICH CHICKEN BROTH

Some swear by it as a cure-all. Others could not cook a week's worth of meals without using it at least once. Making your own chicken broth—especially if you buy whole chickens, cut them up yourself, and reserve the backs, necks, and wings until you have enough for a batch of broth—is a lot more economical than buying the canned kind.

> 2 tablespoons butter or margarine
> 1 medium onion, chopped
> 2 medium leeks, cleaned well and thinly sliced (use part of green tops)
> 1 large carrot, thinly sliced
> 1 stalk celery, with leaves, chopped
> 5 pounds bony chicken pieces (backs, necks, and/or wings)
> 3 sprigs parsley
> ¼ teaspoon each dried thyme and whole peppercorns
> 1 bay leaf
> Pinch dried marjoram
> 4 quarts water
> Salt (optional)

1. In a large, deep kettle (8- to 10-quart size) over medium heat, melt butter. Add onion, leeks, carrot, and celery and cook, stirring often, until onions are soft but not browned. Add chicken pieces, parsley, thyme, peppercorns, bay leaf, marjoram, and the water.

2. Bring slowly to a boil, reduce heat, cover, and simmer until broth has a rich flavor (3½ to 4 hours).

3. Strain broth, discarding solids. Return broth to kettle and boil gently, uncovered, until it is reduced to about 12 cups (30 minutes to 1 hour). Taste, and add salt if desired.

4. If possible, refrigerate broth overnight; then skim off and discard fat. Freeze; or cover and refrigerate, and use within 3 to 4 days.

Makes about 12 cups.

Stockpile beef and chicken bones in the freezer. When you have enough, add vegetables, seasonings, and water and boil into a delicious broth.

Vegetarian Vegetable Broth derives its flavor from an infusion of leeks, carrots, celery, onions, and herbs. Use it as a substitute for meat stocks.

VEGETARIAN VEGETABLE BROTH

This economical soup base tastes good and adds a lot to any soup of which it is a part, although it lacks the intensity and stick-to-the-ribs quality of broth made from chicken or beef bones. You can use it as a substitute for chicken or beef broth in most recipes for puréed or cream soups, or as the cooking liquid in any full-meal soup or stew.

    2 large leeks (about 1½ lbs)
    3 tablespoons butter or
       margarine
    3 large carrots, chopped
    3 stalks celery, with leaves,
       thinly sliced
    2 large onions, chopped
    1 clove garlic, slivered
   12 cups water
    2 teaspoons salt
    5 sprigs parsley
    1 bay leaf
    1 teaspoon dried thyme
    ¼ teaspoon whole black
       peppercorns

1. Cut off root ends of leeks; remove and discard coarse outer leaves. Cut off and discard coarse ends of green tops. Split lengthwise, cutting to within about 1 inch of root end. Soak in cold water for several minutes; then separate leaves under running water to rinse away any clinging grit; drain. Cut cleaned leaks into slices about ¼ inch thick.

2. In an 8-quart kettle over medium heat, melt butter. Add leeks, carrots, celery, onions, and garlic; cook, stirring often, until vegetables are soft but not browned (15 to 20 minutes).

3. Add the water, salt, parsley, bay leaf, thyme, and peppercorns. Bring slowly to a boil. Then cover, reduce heat, and simmer for 2 hours.

4. Strain broth, discarding vegetables and any solids. Let the broth cool, then freeze it. Or cover and refrigerate, and use within 3 to 4 days.

Makes about 10 cups.

FISH BROTH

Many recipes for fish soups, chowders, and seafood stews that call for fish broth suggest bottled clam juice as a possible substitute. Broth is really better because it is more subtle—it gives a gentle marine flavor without obtrusive fishiness.

Most fish dealers will sell you fish scraps—heads and trimmings—for little or nothing. It is best to avoid fat-rich or oily fish when making this broth; that is why salmon is not recommended.

    ¼ cup butter or margarine
    1 large onion, finely chopped
    1 medium carrot, chopped
    1 stalk celery, thinly sliced
    2 to 3 pounds fish bones
       and heads (no salmon)
    8 sprigs parsley
    1 teaspoon whole white
       peppercorns
    ¼ teaspoon dried thyme
    1 bay leaf
    2 cups dry white wine
    6 to 8 cups water

1. In a deep 4- to 6-quart kettle over medium heat, melt butter. Add onion, carrot, and celery and cook, stirring often, until onions are soft but not browned. Add fish, parsley, peppercorns, thyme, bay leaf, and wine. Pour in enough of the water to barely cover fish.

2. Bring slowly to a boil, reduce heat, cover, and simmer for 30 minutes.

3. Strain broth, discarding solids. Taste, and if you wish to concentrate the flavor, boil it gently, uncovered, for 20 to 30 minutes more.

4. Freeze; or cover and refrigerate, and use within 2 days. Remove any solid fat from surface before using.

Makes 6 to 8 cups.

CLEAR SOUPS THAT SPARKLE

Perhaps you believe, as did a character in a short story by Saki, that clear soup is "a more important factor in life than a clear conscience." If so, you may be dissatisfied with broth that has only been strained. Even broth that has been carefully strained through cheesecloth or muslin will still contain enough suspended particles in the liquid to make it appear somewhat cloudy.

The following directions describe the way to transform your homemade chicken or beef stock into sparkling clear broth.

1. *Measure broth. For each 4 cups of broth, beat 2 egg whites (¼ cup) until they are foamy.*

2. *In a large kettle bring the broth to a boil. Whisking constantly, add egg whites. Return to a full boil. Remove from heat and let stand to cool slightly.*

3. *Place a colander over a large bowl. Line the colander with a dampened. well-wrung-out muslin cloth and slowly pour the broth through it. To make sure you get every tasty drop, twist the ends of the cloth and gently press out liquid. Discard solids. Reheat broth and use it at once. If you prefer. cool and refrigerate it for up to 2 days.*

GROWING AND DRYING HERBS

Growing herbs is no more difficult than growing ordinary flowers and vegetables. What's more, the additional flavor that fresh herbs will bring to your soups and stews makes the effort well worthwhile.

Traditionally, herbs were relegated to a separate herb garden. But in an informal setting, gardeners plant low growers such as parsley, chives, dwarf sages, and thymes as borders or among flowering annuals and perennials. They also use creeping thyme as a fragrant ground cover and rosemary to cascade over a retaining wall.

Herbs and spices are good candidates for container gardening. The containers can be placed within easy reach of the kitchen and moved as sun patterns change.

In a sunny window or under artificial light, herbs may keep on growing all winter. They can be moved to planters or beds outdoors when the weather warms up or, if their growing requirements are met, they can remain indoors the year around.

Growing Indoors *If your gardening is limited to the indoors, pick a spot with good sunlight or sufficient artificial light. Use colorful food cans as planters or cachepots and arrange them on a windowsill, or suspend potted herbs in hanging planters in front of a window.*

Planting in Containers *You can pot herbs in any of the various containers designed for growing plants outdoors. Here, a clay strawberry jar is used. Fill the jar with potting soil and plant herbs in the pockets. Use the top as a bed in which to grow red leaf lettuce.*

Planting in Flower Borders *Use herbs as border plants in a bed of bulbs or flowering annuals. Plant them as you would any other potted plant. To get a head start on the season, begin seeds indoors in the winter and transplant them when all danger of frost is past.*

Growing in Baskets *Line a wire basket with green sphagnum moss. Put about 2 inches of soil at the bottom, then poke a small plant through the wire so the roots lie on the surface of the soil and the crown just touches the moss. Continue in this way until the basket is full.*

Formal Herb Gardens *To plant a traditional herb garden, first work it out carefully on paper. Design geometric-shaped beds and define them with a herbal "hedge."*

How to Dry Herbs *The traditional method of drying herbs is to pick branches and arrange them in bunches. Tie each bunch with string, and hang upside down in a warm, dry place away from direct sunlight. To prevent mildew, hang where air can circulate all around. Depending on the weather, drying will take about two weeks.*

A quicker method is to spread the leaves on a cheesecloth-covered rack in an oven set at the lowest temperature. Leave the oven door open and stir the leaves until they are crisp; this will only take a few minutes.

To preserve herbs for use in the winter, just hang them in bunches by their stems. Strip the leaves and store them, or use the bunches as decoration.

French Alpine Soup (see page 32 for the recipe) contains a veritable garden of vegetables. It is one of the light, first-course soups to be found in this chapter.

Super First-Course Soups

For many families, the cheery call "Soup's on!" means it's time to eat. Although the soups in this chapter are on the light side, often you will find them just right for lunch or supper, served with crackers or bread, cheese, a salad, or fruit. Pack one of the soups in a thermos to take on a cool-weather picnic. Suggestions for an entire meal include menus for an after-theater onion soup supper (pages 20-21); a winter lunch with a nippy Cheddar cheese soup (pages 34-35); and a football buffet highlighted by an autumn squash soup (pages 26-27). And why not soup for dessert or breakfast? The fruit soup recipes on page 40 offer some sweet surprises.

Spanish Garlic Soup, followed with a cup of hot tea and fresh fruits, makes a flavorful lunch.

CLEAR SOUPS

Sparkling broth is a culinary classic. Additions of meat, poultry, or vegetables for flavor and color can be as simple or as complex as you choose. Canned stock or bouillon cubes and powders may be used as quick substitutes, but homemade broth (see pages 8–11) is always preferable. Keep it on hand in the freezer.

SPANISH GARLIC SOUP

Poached eggs and bacon enrich this pungently flavored broth. You can serve the soup as the first course of a light dinner with grilled chicken or fish, or you can enjoy it for lunch with fresh fruit.

> 3 thick slices bacon, cut crosswise in thin strips
> 3 tablespoons olive oil
> 8 cloves garlic, sliced
> 1 tablespoon tomato paste

> 3½ cups Sturdy Beef Broth (see page 8) or 2 cans (14½ oz each) regular-strength beef broth
> ½ cup dry sherry
> Salt and pepper
> Fresh cilantro (Chinese parsley) or parsley leaves (optional)

Baguette Croutons

> 8 thin slices French baguette, about ¼ inch thick
> 1 tablespoon butter or margarine
> 1 teaspoon olive oil
> Pinch cayenne pepper

Poached Eggs

> 4 eggs (in shells)

1. Prepare Baguette Croutons.

2. In a heavy 2- to 3-quart saucepan, cook bacon strips until they are crisp and golden brown. Remove bacon pieces with a slotted spoon and drain them well on paper towels. Discard the bacon drippings.

3. In same pan heat olive oil over medium heat. Add garlic and cook, stirring often, until lightly browned. Meanwhile, dilute tomato paste with a little of the broth; add with remaining broth to garlic mixture. Bring to a boil, cover, reduce heat, and simmer for 20 minutes.

4. While soup simmers prepare Poached Eggs.

5. Remove garlic from broth with a slotted spoon; discard garlic. Add sherry to broth. Season with salt and pepper to taste. Reheat until broth begins to boil.

6. To serve, divide hot Baguette Croutons among warm soup bowls. Put a poached egg into each bowl on top of croutons. Pour steaming hot soup over eggs and let stand for about half a minute before serving. Sprinkle each serving with bacon, and with cilantro if you wish.

Makes 4½ to 5 cups, 4 servings.

Baguette Croutons Preheat oven to 300° F. Arrange baguette slices in a single layer on a baking sheet. Melt butter with olive oil; stir in cayenne pepper. Brush butter mixture evenly over bread slices. Bake until crisp and lightly browned (20 to 25 minutes). Reheat just before serving soup.

Makes 8 croutons.

Poached Eggs Immerse eggs in rapidly boiling water for 5 seconds; remove eggs and set them aside. Pour water into a large, deep frying pan to a depth of about 2½ inches; place over high heat until water begins to boil. Then adjust heat so that water barely bubbles. Break eggs directly into water and cook gently until whites are firm (2 to 3 minutes). Remove poached eggs from cooking water with a slotted spoon and serve at once, or immerse them in a bowl of very cold water. If cooked ahead, cover and refrigerate; to reheat eggs, transfer to a bowl of water that is just hot to the touch and let stand 5 to 10 minutes. Just before serving transfer eggs to soup bowls as directed.

BEEFY RED WINE AND TOMATO SOUP

Noodlelike strips of parsley-flavored pancakes are an intriguing garnish.

- 3½ cups Sturdy Beef Broth (see page 8) or 2 cans (14½ oz each) regular-strength beef broth
- 2 medium tomatoes, peeled, seeded, and chopped
- 1 tablespoon lemon juice
  Parsleyed Pancake Strips (see page 76)
- ½ cup dry red wine
  Salt and pepper

1. In a 2- to 3-quart enamel saucepan, combine broth, tomatoes, and lemon juice. Bring to a boil over medium heat. Cover, reduce heat, and simmer for 25 minutes. Meanwhile, make Parsleyed Pancake Strips.

2. Gradually stir wine into soup. Reheat until steaming hot. Taste, and add salt and pepper as needed.

3. Divide pancake strips among 4 or 5 soup bowls. Add hot soup.

Makes 5½ cups, 4 or 5 servings.

CHICKEN SOUP WITH LENTILS

Lentil soup can be a stick-to-the-ribs affair. This version is not so filling.

- 2 tablespoons butter or margarine
- 1 small onion, thinly slivered
- ¼ cup each *finely chopped celery and fresh parsley*
- 1 medium carrot, shredded
- ½ cup dried lentils, rinsed and drained
- ⅛ teaspoon white pepper
  Pinch ground cloves
- 5 cups Rich Chicken Broth (see page 8) or 3 cans (14½ oz each) chicken broth
  Salt (optional)

1. In a 2- to 3-quart saucepan over medium heat, melt butter. Add onion, celery, parsley, and carrot. Cook, stirring often, until vegetables are soft but not browned. Add lentils, pepper, cloves, and broth.

2. Bring soup to a boil, cover, and reduce heat. Stirring occasionally so lentils don't stick to the bottom, boil gently until lentils are tender (25 to 30 minutes).

3. Taste, and add salt if needed.

Makes about 6 cups, 4 to 6 servings.

DOUBLE MUSHROOM SOUP WITH BARLEY

Fresh ginger hints of the Orient in this easy soup that combines fresh Japanese tree oyster mushrooms with the more familiar cultivated kind.

- ¼ cup butter or margarine
- 1 package (4 oz) fresh tree oyster or other Japanese-type mushrooms (small mushrooms whole, larger ones slivered)
- ¼ pound cultivated mushrooms, thinly sliced
- ¼ cup pearl barley, rinsed and drained
- 1 small clove garlic, minced or pressed
- 3½ cups Sturdy Beef Broth (see page 8) or 2 cans (14½ oz each) regular-strength beef broth
- 1 teaspoon grated fresh ginger or ¼ teaspoon ground ginger
  Salt and white pepper
- 2 green onions, thinly sliced on the diagonal

1. In a heavy 2- to 3-quart saucepan over medium heat, melt butter. Add both kinds of mushrooms and cook, stirring occasionally, until they are lightly browned and any liquid has cooked away. Add barley and garlic, stirring to coat barley with mushroom mixture.

2. Mix in 1 cup of the broth. Bring to a boil, cover, reduce heat, and simmer until barley is tender (about 45 minutes).

3. Stir in ginger and remaining broth. Cook, uncovered, over medium heat until soup is hot. Taste, add salt if needed, and pepper to taste. Just before serving, stir in onions.

Makes 4 cups, 4 servings.

Colored by tomatoes and spiced with hot chiles, garlic, and cumin, this Taxco Miners' Soup can be turned into a meal when followed by grilled fish.

TAXCO MINERS' SOUP

Hot, crisply fried tortilla strips sizzle as this zesty Mexican soup is ladled over them. After the soup, serve grilled snapper or shrimp with garlic butter, and a green vegetable.

> *Salad oil, for frying*
> 4 *corn tortillas (6-in. diam), cut in halves, then into ½-inch-wide strips*
> *Salt*
> 1 *tablespoon olive oil or salad oil*
> 1 *medium onion, thinly slivered*
> 1 *small clove garlic, minced or pressed*
> ½ *teaspoon ground cumin*
> 2 *canned green chiles, finely chopped*
> 1 *large can (15 oz) tomato sauce*
> 2 *cups Rich Chicken Broth (see page 8) or 1 can (14½ oz) chicken broth*
> 1 *cup water*
> ¼ *pound jack cheese, cut in ½-inch cubes (about 1 cup)*
> *Sour cream, for garnish (optional)*

1. Pour salad oil into a deep, heavy frying pan to a depth of about ½ inch. Heat to a temperature of 350° to 375° F. Fry tortilla strips, about a third at a time, until crisp and lightly browned (about 2 minutes). Remove with a slotted spoon to paper towels to drain. Salt lightly.

2. Heat the olive oil in a 2- to 3-quart saucepan over medium heat. Add onion and cook, stirring, until soft but not browned. Mix in garlic and cumin; then add green chiles, tomato sauce, broth, and the water. Bring to a boil, cover, reduce heat, and simmer for 10 minutes.

3. Meanwhile, spread tortilla strips in a shallow pan and heat in a 325° F oven for 8 to 10 minutes. Place heatproof soup bowls on a baking sheet in oven during last 5 minutes.

4. With pot holders, remove hot soup bowls to a heatproof tray. Working quickly, divide hot tortilla strips among the bowls. Top with cheese cubes. Ladle hot soup over tortillas and cheese and serve at once.

5. Spoon in a little sour cream at the table, if desired.

Makes 6 to 8 cups, 4 servings.

DANISH OXTAIL CONSOMMÉ

The origin of this beautiful amber broth is the humble but flavorful oxtail. Simmered slowly for rich flavor and then clarified, it makes a subtly elegant first course with the addition of tiny meat dumplings and a splash of Madeira.

> 2½ *to 3 pounds oxtails, cut in segments*
> 8 *cups water*
> 2 *medium carrots*
> 1 *large onion, chopped*
> 1 *clove garlic, slivered*
> ¼ *teaspoon each dried thyme and whole black peppercorns*
> 3 *sprigs parsley*
> 1 *bay leaf*
> 2 *tablespoons tomato paste*
> 4 *egg whites (about ½ cup)*
> 1 *medium leek*
> *Salt (optional)*
> *Danish Meat Dumplings (see page 76)*
> 3 *tablespoons Madeira or sherry*

1. Preheat oven to 450° F. Place oxtails in a shallow baking pan in a single layer. Bake, uncovered, until meat is well browned (25 to 30 minutes).

2. Transfer oxtails to a deep 5- to 6-quart kettle. Add a little of the water to roasting pan, stirring to dissolve brown drippings. Add to oxtails. Chop 1 of the carrots and add to oxtails with onion, garlic, thyme, peppercorns, parsley, bay leaf, and tomato paste. Add the remaining water. Bring to a boil and cover. Reduce heat and simmer until the meat is extremely tender and the broth is richly flavored (3 to 4 hours).

3. Strain broth; discard solids, reserving meat for other uses if you wish. (This can be done ahead; refrigerate broth until ready to complete soup.) Skim and discard fat.

4. Return broth to a clean kettle. Bring to a boil and clarify with egg whites as directed on page 11. Strain as directed and return to a clean kettle. Reheat.

5. Cut remaining carrot lengthwise into quarters; then thinly slice crosswise. Cut off root end of leek; remove coarse outer leaves. Cut off and discard dark green top. Split leek lengthwise, from leafy end, cutting to within about 1 inch of root end. Soak in cold water for several minutes; then separate leaves under running water to rinse away any clinging grit. Drain, and cut leek into slices about ¼ inch thick.

6. Add vegetables to hot clarified broth and cook, covered, over medium heat, until vegetables are tender-crisp (about 5 minutes). Taste, and add salt if needed. Add Danish Meat Dumplings and heat through. Stir in Madeira and heat for about 1 minute longer. Serve hot.

Makes 6 to 8 cups, 6 servings.

LATE EVENING SOUP SUPPER

Onion Soup With Beer

Dilled Lettuce, Tomato, and Cucumber Salad

Mocha-Almond Ice Cream Pie

Beer or Red Jug Wine

Coffee

When you come home hungry after the theater, a movie, or an evening sporting event, this is the soup to have waiting.

To prepare the supper in advance, complete the soup through step 3; shred and refrigerate the Swiss cheese. When you're ready to serve, add the remaining broth, reheat, and broil the soup in individual serving bowls with the topping.

ONION SOUP WITH BEER

6 *medium onions (2 to 2½ lbs)*
⅓ *cup butter or margarine*
2 *cloves garlic*
3 *tablespoons flour*
1 *teaspoon paprika*
1 *bottle or can (12 oz) dark beer*
8 *cups Sturdy Beef Broth (see page 8) or canned regular-strength beef broth*
6 *to 8 slices French bread, cut about 1 inch thick*
6 *to 8 tablespoons grated Parmesan cheese*
Salt and pepper
½ *to ¾ pound Swiss cheese, shredded (2 to 3 cups)*

1. Cut onions in half lengthwise, then into lengthwise slivers. In a 5- to 6-quart kettle over medium heat, melt butter. Add onions, cover, and cook until limp (about 10 minutes). Uncover and cook, stirring often, until onions brown lightly (about 15 minutes). Reduce heat to medium-low if onions begin to brown too quickly.

2. Mince or press 1 of the garlic cloves. Add the minced garlic, flour, and paprika to onions, stirring to blend flour into mixture. Remove from heat and gradually stir in beer and 2 cups of the broth. Return to heat and bring to a boil, stirring. Cover, reduce heat, and simmer for 1 hour.

3. Meanwhile, place bread slices on a baking sheet. Peel remaining clove of garlic, cut it in half, and with it rub both sides of each bread slice. Bake in 325° F oven until crisp and lightly browned (40 to 45 minutes). Sprinkle each slice with 1 tablespoon of the Parmesan cheese.

4. After soup has simmered for 1 hour, add remaining 6 cups broth; bring to a gentle boil. Season to taste.

5. Divide soup among 6 or 8 oven-proof bowls. Top each with a slice of toasted French bread. Divide Swiss cheese evenly and sprinkle over bread slices. Place bowls on a baking sheet about 6 inches below broiler. Broil until the cheese is bubbling and lightly browned (6 to 8 minutes). Serve at once.

Makes 10 to 12 cups, 6 to 8 servings.

DILLED LETTUCE, TOMATO, AND CUCUMBER SALAD

1 *small cucumber*
10 *cups torn butter or Boston lettuce*
1 *cup cherry tomatoes, cut in halves*

Dill Dressing

2 *tablespoons white wine vinegar*
2 *teaspoons lemon juice*
1½ *teaspoons Dijon mustard*
1 *clove garlic, minced or pressed*
½ *teaspoon dried dill weed*
⅛ *teaspoon salt*
Pinch coarsely ground black pepper
2 *tablespoons olive oil*
⅓ *cup salad oil*

1. Peel cucumber, cut in half lengthwise, and scoop out and discard seeds. Slice thinly.

2. In a large salad bowl, combine cucumber, lettuce, and tomatoes.

3. Make Dill Dressing; pour over salad and mix lightly.

Serves 6 to 8.

Dill Dressing In a medium bowl mix vinegar, lemon juice, mustard, garlic, dill weed, salt, and pepper. Using a whisk or fork, gradually mix in oil until blended and slightly thickened.

Makes about ½ cup.

MOCHA-ALMOND ICE CREAM PIE

- ½ cup each *toasted slivered almonds and firmly packed brown sugar*
- 2 *tablespoons butter or margarine, melted*
- ½ cup *coarsely chopped semisweet chocolate*
- 1 *quart coffee ice cream, softened*
- 1 *teaspoon salad oil*

Chocolate Chip Crust

- ⅓ cup *butter or margarine, softened*
- ¼ cup *firmly packed brown sugar*
- ½ teaspoon *vanilla extract*
- 1 *egg yolk*
- 1 *cup flour*
- ¼ cup *finely chopped semisweet chocolate*

1. Prepare Chocolate Chip Crust.

2. In a medium bowl mix almonds, brown sugar, and butter. Add ¼ cup of the chocolate and mix lightly.

3. Spread half of the ice cream in cooled crust. Sprinkle evenly with half of the almond mixture. Cover with remaining ice cream, then remaining almond mixture. Freeze.

4. Place remaining ¼ cup chopped chocolate over hot (but not boiling) water until melted. Stir in salad oil. Drizzle over top of partially frozen pie using a spoon or a cone of rolled paper. Return pie to freezer.

5. When top is set, cover with foil. Freeze 3 to 4 hours or overnight.

6. Remove pie from freezer and let stand in refrigerator for about 30 minutes before cutting.

Serves 6 to 8.

Chocolate Chip Crust Preheat oven to 375° F. In a medium bowl combine butter and brown sugar; beat until fluffy. Beat in vanilla, then egg yolk. Gradually blend in flour until mixture is combined. Blend in chocolate. Press mixture firmly over bottom and up sides of a 9-inch pie pan. Pierce in several places with a fork. Bake until lightly browned (12 to 14 minutes). Cool in pan on a wire rack.

Onion soup, bubbly from the broiler, stars at a late supper after a night at the opera. Under the toasted French bread topped with melted Swiss cheese is a savory broth spiked with beer. Serve additional beer to sip with the soup.

Sweet red peppers, sautéed then puréed, are featured in colorful Red Pepper Soup. The soup can be easily prepared in a little over half an hour.

PURÉED SOUPS

When you cook vegetables in broth and then whirl them in a blender or food processor, the result is a smooth, naturally thickened soup. Such soups have an inherent elegance as first courses. Most are complemented by a topping of buttery homemade croutons (see page 76).

RED PEPPER SOUP

You will enjoy the distinctive flavor of sweet red peppers in this soup, as well as its brilliant scarlet color.

> 3 tablespoons butter or margarine
> 3 large red bell peppers (about 1¼ lbs), seeded and chopped
> 1 medium onion, finely chopped
> ¼ teaspoon ground cumin
> Pinch cayenne pepper
> 3½ cups Rich Chicken Broth (see page 8) or 2 cans (14½ oz each) chicken broth
> 2 teaspoons lemon juice
> Salt (optional)
> Few sprigs Italian (flat-leaf) parsley, for garnish

1. In a 3-quart saucepan over medium heat, melt butter. Add bell peppers and onion and cook, stirring occasionally, until onion is soft but not browned. Mix in cumin and cayenne; then add chicken broth.

2. Bring to a boil, cover, reduce heat, and simmer for 20 minutes.

3. With a slotted spoon, scoop out vegetables and transfer to a blender or food processor. Add a little of the broth and whirl or process until smooth. Return red pepper purée to broth in cooking pan. Mix in lemon juice. Taste, and add salt if needed.

4. Reheat to serving temperature. Serve hot, garnishing each serving with a few leaves of parsley.

Makes 5½ cups, 4 or 5 servings.

BASIL AND SPINACH SOUP WITH LEMON CREAM

Fresh basil is the flavor secret of this soup finished with a dollop of lemony whipped cream.

> 2 bunches spinach (about 1½ lbs)
> 3 tablespoons olive oil or fat skimmed from the chicken broth
> 1 medium onion, finely chopped
> 1 clove garlic, minced or pressed
> 1 cup lightly packed fresh basil leaves
> 3½ cups Rich Chicken Broth (see page 8) or 2 cans (14½ oz each) chicken broth
> ½ cup grated Parmesan cheese
> 1 cup whipping cream
> Salt (optional)
> 2 teaspoons lemon juice
> ¼ teaspoon grated lemon rind

1. Rinse spinach well, drain, and remove and discard stems. (You should have about 16 cups leaves, lightly packed.)

2. In a 4- to 5-quart kettle, heat olive oil over medium heat. Add onion and cook until soft but not browned. Mix in garlic. Then add spinach and basil leaves, stirring often until leaves wilt.

3. Add broth. Bring to a boil, reduce heat, and simmer, uncovered, for 10 minutes.

4. With a slotted spoon, scoop out spinach and basil and transfer to a blender or food processor. Add a little of the broth and whirl or process until smooth. Return purée to pan.

5. Mix in cheese and ⅔ cup of the whipping cream. Reheat to serving temperature; taste, and add salt if needed.

6. In a medium bowl combine remaining ⅓ cup cream with lemon juice and lemon rind. Beat until stiff. Spoon a little of the lemon cream over each serving of the hot soup.

Makes about 7 cups, 4 to 6 servings.

PURÉEING

Producing a smooth, creamy soup out of vegetables and broth used to be a time-consuming, laborious, and messy job. Today, puréeing is something the well-equipped cook can do in a snap by enlisting the aid of either a blender or a food processor.

Food Processors *Many cooks consider this multi-function machine their most valuable kitchen appliance. It will chop, slice, shred, and mix as well as purée. These abilities make it ideal for a recipe that calls for a variety of chopped vegetables to be sautéed and then puréed. With soups, you don't even have to wash out the work bowl between tasks.*

The machine is so fast that control of the speed is critical. Proper technique makes the difference between chopped onions and onion purée.

Blenders *In terms of overall versatility, the blender suffers when it is compared to a food processor. However, for puréeing a soup, it works equally well. In fact, for puréeing small amounts, the tall, narrow container is more efficient than the wider processor bowl.*

Blenders may have as many as 16 speeds, including an on-off pulse action designed to give more control over food consistency.

SHERRIED BLACK BEAN SOUP

An assortment of toppings allows guests to accent this suave bean soup.

1 pound dried black beans, rinsed and drained
8 cups water
2 tablespoons butter or margarine
2 medium onions, chopped
1 stalk celery, thinly sliced
1 medium carrot, shredded
1 clove garlic, minced or pressed
1 ham hock (about 1 lb)
¼ cup chopped fresh parsley
1 teaspoon salt
⅛ teaspoon each cayenne pepper, whole cloves, and mustard seed
1 bay leaf
⅓ cup dry sherry
Thinly sliced green onions, crumbled crisp bacon, sour cream, sieved hard-cooked egg, and thin lemon slices, for garnish

1. In a large, heavy saucepan, bring beans and 4 cups of the water to a boil. Boil briskly for 2 minutes; then remove from heat and let stand, covered, for 1 hour.

2. In a 5-quart Dutch oven, melt butter. Add onions, celery, carrot, and garlic, and cook until soft but not browned. Add ham hock, remaining 4 cups water, parsley, salt, cayenne, cloves, mustard seed, bay leaf, and beans (with their liquid). Bring to a boil, cover, reduce heat, and simmer for about 3 hours.

3. Remove ham hock and let cool slightly. Remove and discard bay leaf. Place about half of the beans with about 1 cup of the liquid from the soup in a blender or food processor. Whirl or process until smooth. Return purée to soup in Dutch oven.

4. Remove ham from bone and add meat to soup. (Discard fat, bones, and skin.) Reheat soup over medium heat. Stir in sherry.

5. Serve hot soup with choice of garnishes to sprinkle on top.

Makes 8 to 10 cups. 8 servings.

ORANGE AND TOMATO SOUP

Orange rind and juice accent an easy-to-make tomato soup from the Chelsea section of London. Follow the soup with broiled lamb chops, broccoli, and a crusty gratin of potatoes.

2 tablespoons butter or margarine
1 small onion, finely chopped
1 small clove garlic, minced or pressed
¼ teaspoon ground cumin
⅛ teaspoon white pepper
1 large can (28 oz) tomatoes
Grated rind and juice of 1 large orange
1¾ cups Rich Chicken Broth (see page 8) or 1 can (14½ oz) chicken broth
Salt (optional)
Sour cream and additional grated orange rind, for garnish

1. In a 3- to 4-quart saucepan over medium heat, melt butter. Add onion and cook until soft but not browned. Mix in garlic, cumin, and pepper. Then add tomatoes (break up with a fork) and their liquid. Mix in orange rind and juice and chicken broth.

2. Bring to a boil, cover, reduce heat, and simmer for 30 minutes.

3. In a blender or food processor, whirl or process soup, about half at a time, until smooth. Return purée to cooking pan; taste, and add salt if needed.

4. Reheat to serving temperature. Serve hot, garnishing each serving with a dollop of sour cream and a sprinkling of orange rind.

Makes 6½ cups. 4 to 6 servings.

CREAMY SOUPS

Adding milk, half-and-half, or cream to a puréed soup changes its character considerably. Not only does the soup become silkier and seem more special, its nutritional profile also expands with the addition of protein and calcium.

FRENCH CREAM OF MUSHROOM SOUP

Thick, and savory with herbs, this fresh mushroom soup will lure you away from its pallid canned counterpart forever.

¼ cup butter or margarine
1 pound mushrooms, thinly sliced
2 shallots, finely chopped (about ¼ cup)
1 tablespoon flour
½ teaspoon each salt and dried savory
Pinch white pepper
2 teaspoons tomato paste
2 cups Sturdy Beef Broth (see page 8) or 1 can (14½ oz) regular-strength beef broth
1 tablespoon lemon juice
2 cups half-and-half
2 tablespoons dry vermouth

1. In a 3-quart pan over moderately high heat, melt butter. Add mushrooms and shallots and cook, stirring often, until mushrooms brown lightly and most of their liquid is gone.

2. Sprinkle with flour, salt, savory, and pepper. Add tomato paste; stir mushrooms to coat with added ingredients. Remove from heat and gradually blend in beef broth. Bring to a boil, cover, reduce heat, and simmer for 20 minutes.

3. Purée mushroom mixture in blender or food processor until smooth, mixing in lemon juice at end. Return to cooking pan, blend in half-and-half, and stir often over medium heat until steaming hot. *Do not boil.* Taste, and add salt if needed.

4. Add vermouth and serve at once.

Makes about 5 cups. 4 servings.

PERUVIAN CREOLE SOUP

The loin pork chop is included more as a flavoring rather than a main ingredient of *sopa de criolla*, a favorite opening for a light meal of grilled chicken or fish.

Be careful when handling chiles: they can burn the skin. Keep your hands away from your face, especially your eyes. The hottest part of a chile is the placental tissue that connects the seed to the walls, so cleaning chiles exposes you more than do other operations. If you are going to handle many chiles or if you have tender skin, wear rubber gloves.

> 1 *loin pork chop, about ¾ inch thick (about ½ lb)*
> 1 *to 2 teaspoons salad oil*
> 1 *medium onion, finely chopped*
> 1 *medium tomato, peeled, seeded, and chopped*
> 1 *small dried hot red chile, finely crushed*
> 1 *small clove garlic, minced or pressed*
> ½ *teaspoon each salt and ground cumin*
> ¼ *teaspoon ground turmeric*
> 3½ *cups Rich Chicken Broth (see page 8) or 2 cans (14½ oz each) chicken broth*
> 2 *egg yolks*
> 1 *cup half-and-half Chopped parsley, for garnish*

1. Trim fat from pork chop. Cut this fat into small pieces, and reserve it. Cut the meat from the bone and discard the bone. Cut meat into thin, bite-sized strips.

2. In a 3-quart saucepan over medium heat, cook pork fat until it coats pan; add a little salad oil if needed. Discard any solid pieces of fat. Add pork strips and onion and cook, stirring, until lightly browned. Mix in tomato, chile, garlic, salt, cumin, and turmeric.

3. Add broth, bring to a boil, cover, reduce heat, and simmer until pork is very tender (about 30 minutes). Meanwhile, in a small bowl beat egg yolks with half-and-half.

4. After 30 minutes, gradually whisk about 1 cup of the hot broth into egg mixture; stir it vigorously into soup and continue stirring over medium-low heat until soup is steaming hot and slightly thickened. *Do not boil.* Taste, and add salt if needed.

5. Serve sprinkled with parsley.

Makes about 5½ cups, 4 servings.

Whole chiles, mild or hot, will dry in several weeks at room temperature. When they are dry, crumble or grind them for use in Peruvian Creole Soup, the chili recipes on pages 88 and 89, and other spicy-hot dishes.

25

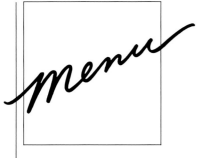

FOOTBALL BUFFET

Golden Squash Soup

Open-Faced Ham Sandwiches on Braided Oatmeal Bread

Bread-and-Butter Pickles

Radishes and Celery Sticks

Apple Upside-Down Cake

Beer or Cider

Coffee

Before or after the game, offer soup and sandwiches. The bread recipe produces two loaves—one for this menu and a second one to freeze. The soup can be made through step 2, covered, and refrigerated. The cake is best served warm. If you bake it in advance, cover it lightly with foil and reheat in a 325° F oven for 15 to 20 minutes.

GOLDEN SQUASH SOUP

- 1 *piece (1½ lbs) winter squash*
- 2 *tablespoons butter or margarine*
- 1 *small onion, finely chopped*
- 1 *tablespoon flour*
- 2 *tablespoons chunky peanut butter*
- 2 *cups Rich Chicken Broth (see page 8) or 1 can (14½ oz) chicken broth*
- ½ *teaspoon each salt and dry mustard*
  Pinch each white pepper and cayenne pepper
- 2 *cups milk*
  Sour cream, for garnish

1. Preheat oven to 400° F. Place squash cut side down in a greased baking dish, cover, and bake until very tender (40 to 50 minutes). Scoop out squash and discard rind. (You should have approximately 2 cups cooked squash.) Purée in a blender or food processor, or press through a food mill.

2. In a 3-quart saucepan over medium heat, melt butter. Add onion and cook until soft but not browned. Blend in flour, then peanut butter. Remove from heat and gradually blend in chicken broth. Blend in puréed squash, salt, dry mustard, pepper, and cayenne. Cook, stirring, until mixture thickens and boils.

3. Blend in milk and heat to serving temperature. Serve topped with dollops of sour cream.

Makes 6 to 7 cups, 4 to 6 servings.

BRAIDED OATMEAL BREAD

- 1 *cup rolled oats*
- 1 *cup boiling water*
- 1 *cup milk*
- 3 *tablespoons butter or margarine*
- ¼ *cup honey*
- 2 *teaspoons salt*
- 1 *envelope active dry yeast*
- ¼ *cup warm water*
- 4½ *to 5 cups unbleached flour*
- 1 *cup wheat germ*
- 1 *egg yolk, beaten with 1 teaspoon water*
- 2 *tablespoons rolled oats*

1. Place the 1 cup rolled oats in a medium bowl, pour on the boiling water, and let stand until mixture is lukewarm.

2. Scald milk in a small pan; remove from heat and add butter, honey, and salt. Stir until butter melts.

3. In large bowl of an electric mixer, sprinkle yeast over the warm water; let stand until soft (about 5 minutes). To yeast mixture add cooled oatmeal mixture, milk mixture, and 3 cups of the flour. Mix to blend; then beat at medium speed until smooth and elastic (about 5 minutes). Stir in wheat germ and about 1 cup more flour to make a stiff dough.

4. Turn dough out onto a board or pastry cloth floured generously with some of the remaining ½ to 1 cup flour. Knead until dough is smooth and springy and small bubbles form just under the surface (10 to 15 minutes), adding more flour as required to prevent dough from being too sticky.

5. Turn dough in a greased bowl. Cover and let rise in a warm place until doubled (1 to 1½ hours). Punch dough down and divide it in half. Divide each portion into 3 pieces.

6. On a lightly floured surface, roll each piece to a 15-inch-long strand. Place 3 of the strands side by side and braid, being careful not to stretch dough. Pinch ends to seal. Repeat with remaining 3 strands. Place each braid in a greased 4½- by 8½-inch loaf pan. Cover lightly and let rise until almost doubled (45 minutes to 1 hour).

7. Preheat oven to 350° F. Brush egg mixture lightly over each braid. Sprinkle each loaf evenly with 1 tablespoon rolled oats. Bake loaves until they are well browned and sound hollow when they are tapped lightly (45 to 50 minutes). Remove to wire racks to cool.

Makes 2 loaves.

APPLE UPSIDE-DOWN CAKE

> ¾ cup butter or margarine
> 1½ cups firmly packed light brown sugar
> 2 small tart cooking apples, peeled, cored, and thinly sliced
> 1¾ cups flour
> 2½ teaspoons baking powder
> 1 teaspoon ground cinnamon
> ¼ teaspoon each salt and ground nutmeg
> ⅛ teaspoon ground cloves
> 1 egg
> 1 teaspoon vanilla extract
> 1 cup milk
> Whipped cream (optional)

1. Preheat oven to 350° F. In a 9-inch square or 10-inch round baking pan over low heat, melt ¼ cup of the butter. (Set remaining butter aside to soften.) Add ½ cup of the brown sugar and cook, stirring constantly, until mixture bubbles all over (5 to 10 minutes). Remove from heat and arrange apple slices evenly in sugar mixture; set aside.

2. In a medium bowl blend flour, baking powder, cinnamon, salt, nutmeg, and cloves.

3. Beat the remaining ½ cup butter with remaining 1 cup brown sugar until light and fluffy. Beat in egg, then vanilla. Add flour mixture to butter mixture alternately with milk, mixing until smooth after each addition. Spread evenly over apples in prepared pan.

4. Bake until cake is well browned and tests done when a wooden toothpick is inserted near center (50 to 55 minutes).

5. While cake is still warm, loosen edges with a spatula and turn out onto a serving plate. Cut in squares or wedges. Serve warm, with whipped cream, if desired.

Serves 6 to 8.

If pressed for time, set out thinly sliced Westphalian or baked ham, lettuce, and mayonnaise or a seasoned butter (add a little horse-radish and Dijon mustard to softened butter). Then let guests make their own sandwiches.

CLEANING HARD-SHELL CRABS

1. *Gently fold back the apron or tail flap; twist and pull it off. (The intestinal vein is attached and will pull out together with the apron. Discard both.) Pry up, tear off, and discard the top shell.*

2. *Remove gills from each side of the crab. Pull out and discard the grayish sand bag and the antennae between the eyes.*

3. *Break crab in half, then twist off the claws. Remove meat from the body with your fingers or a knife. Crack claws with a nutcracker and extract meat.*

DUNGENESS CRAB BISQUE

When crab is in season, celebrate with this lusciously creamy soup.

> 1 medium Dungeness crab (about 2 lbs), cooked, cleaned, and cracked
> 4 cups Fish Broth (see page 11) or Rich Chicken Broth (see page 8) or canned chicken broth
> 2 sprigs parsley
> 2 medium onions, thinly sliced
> 1 cup dry white wine
> ¼ cup butter or margarine
> ¼ teaspoon dried tarragon
> ¼ cup flour
> ⅛ teaspoon white pepper
>   Pinch ground nutmeg
> 1 cup half-and-half
> ½ cup whipping cream
>   Salt (optional)
> 3 tablespoons brandy

1. Remove crab from shell, reserving shell. (You should have about 2½ cups crab.)

2. In a 3-quart saucepan combine crab shell, broth, parsley, 1 of the sliced onions, and wine. Bring to a boil over medium heat, cover, reduce heat, and simmer for 30 minutes. Strain through a fine sieve or several thicknesses of dampened cheesecloth.

3. In same 3-quart pan over medium heat, melt butter. Add tarragon and remaining sliced onion and cook, stirring often, until onion is soft but not browned. Stir in crab; cook about 2 minutes. Reserve about ½ cup of the larger pieces of crab.

4. To remaining crab mixture in pan, add flour, pepper, and nutmeg; stir until bubbling. Gradually blend in strained broth. Bring to a boil, cover, reduce heat, and simmer 15 minutes. Transfer to a blender or food processor. Whirl or process until smoothly puréed. Return to cooking pan.

5. Stir in half-and-half. Cook, stirring often, until steaming hot. *Do not boil.* Add cream, reserved crab, and salt if needed; reheat. Just before serving, mix in brandy.

Makes about 6½ cups, 6 servings.

BONGO BONGO SOUP

Inspired by a soup served at Trader Vic's many restaurants, Bongo Bongo is a smooth purée of fresh oysters and spinach. For the finishing touch, spoon whipped cream on top of each serving and broil.

> 1 bunch (about 12 oz) spinach
> 3 tablespoons butter or margarine
> 1 small clove garlic, minced or pressed
> 2 cups milk
> 1 jar (10 fl oz) fresh oysters
> 1 cup whipping cream
> 1 teaspoon Worcestershire sauce
> ¾ teaspoon salt
> ⅛ teaspoon white pepper

1. Remove and discard stems from well-washed spinach. (You should have about 8 cups leaves.) Place spinach in a large saucepan and stir, uncovered, over medium heat with no added liquid until spinach is limp (3 to 5 minutes). Drain well, pressing out excess moisture. Chop spinach coarsely and set it aside.

2. In a 2- to 3-quart saucepan over medium heat, melt butter. Add garlic and cook, stirring, until golden. (Do not brown.) Add milk and heat until it steams. Add oysters (with any liquid) and poach until edges ruffle (2 to 3 minutes). Remove from heat.

3. Transfer oyster mixture to a blender or food processor. Add cooked spinach. Whirl until very smooth.

4. Return spinach and oyster mixture to cooking pan. Add ⅔ cup of the cream and the Worcestershire sauce, salt, and pepper. Stir occasionally over medium heat until blended and steaming hot. *Do not boil.*

5. Whip remaining ⅓ cup cream until not quite stiff. Divide soup among heatproof bowls. Spoon on whipped cream. Broil about 4 inches from heat until golden brown (2 to 3 minutes). Serve immediately.

Makes about 5 cups, 4 servings.

The whipped cream topping spooned onto bowls of savory Bongo Bongo Soup just before serving turns a golden brown under the broiler.

A DANISH-STYLE DINNER

Danish Asparagus and Chicken Soup

Broiled Salmon With Orange-Mint Butter

Whole Green Beans

New Potatoes

Copenhagen-Style Ginger Sundaes

Pretzel-Shaped Butter Cookies

White Wine

Coffee

A velvety, pale green soup sets the festive mood for a candlelit dinner for four. A citrus-and-mint-flavored butter seasons the salmon steaks as they broil.

The tender little butter cookies are packaged or from a Scandinavian bakery. A dry California Fumé Blanc is a good wine to accompany both the soup and the salmon.

DANISH ASPARAGUS AND CHICKEN SOUP

　¾　*pound asparagus*
　3　*tablespoons butter or margarine*
　1　*medium onion, finely chopped*
　1½　*tablespoons flour*
　⅛　*teaspoon dried tarragon Pinch each ground nutmeg and white pepper*
　1　*cup half-and-half*
　1　*egg, slightly beaten*
　2　*teaspoons lemon juice Salt (optional)*

Chicken Breast and Broth

　1　*whole chicken breast (about 1 lb), cut in 2 pieces*
　1　*stalk celery, thinly sliced*
　1　*small onion, chopped*
　2　*whole allspice*
　1　*teaspoon salt*
　3　*cups water*

1. Prepare Chicken Breast and Broth; set meat and broth aside separately.

2. Break off and discard tough ends of asparagus. Cut off tips and cook them, uncovered, in boiling salted water just until tender-crisp (2 to 3 minutes); drain and set aside. Slice remaining asparagus stems about ½ inch thick.

3. In a 3-quart saucepan over medium heat, melt butter. Add onion and cook until soft but not browned. Mix in flour; cook until bubbly. Add tarragon, nutmeg, and pepper. Remove from heat and gradually blend in reserved chicken broth. Cook, stirring, until soup boils gently. Add asparagus stems.

4. Reduce heat, cover, and simmer until asparagus is tender (10 to 12 minutes). Transfer mixture to blender or food processor and whirl or process until smooth. Return asparagus purée to cooking pan.

5. Stir in half-and-half and reserved chicken breast. Cook, stirring, over medium heat until soup is steaming hot. In a small bowl beat egg with lemon juice. Stir in a little of the hot soup; then blend egg mixture into hot soup. Cook, stirring, until hot but not boiling. Taste, and add salt if needed. Garnish with reserved asparagus tips. Serve soup steaming hot.

Makes about 5 cups, 4 servings.

Chicken Breast and Broth In a 2- to 3-quart saucepan combine chicken, celery, onion, allspice, salt, and water. Bring to a boil, cover, reduce heat, and simmer for 45 minutes. Strain, reserving broth. Discard seasonings, bones, and skin. Cut chicken into thin, bite-sized pieces.

BROILED SALMON WITH ORANGE-MINT BUTTER

　½　*cup butter or margarine, softened*
　½　*teaspoon each grated orange and lemon rind*
　1　*tablespoon each orange and lemon juice*
　¼　*cup finely chopped fresh mint leaves or 1 tablespoon dried mint*
　⅛　*teaspoon white pepper*
　4　*salmon steaks, ¾ to 1 inch thick Salad oil*

1. In a medium bowl beat butter until fluffy. Add orange and lemon rinds; then gradually beat in orange and lemon juices until well combined. Blend in mint and pepper. Cover and refrigerate butter mixture to blend flavors (2 to 3 hours or overnight).

2. Remove butter from refrigerator to soften slightly while preparing salmon. Brush salmon steaks lightly with oil on both sides. Brush broiler rack lightly with oil. Arrange salmon steaks, slightly apart, on rack. Broil, 4 inches from heat, for 4 minutes.

3. Broil, about 4 inches from heat, for 4 minutes. Turn salmon and dot each steak with a generous teaspoon of the orange-mint butter. Broil until salmon browns lightly and flakes easily when tested with a fork (4 to 5 minutes).

4. Serve salmon with additional orange-mint butter for each serving.

Serves 4.

COPENHAGEN-STYLE GINGER SUNDAES

¼ cup preserved ginger in syrup
2 tablespoons syrup from preserved ginger
⅓ cup white crème de cacao
8 generous scoops rich vanilla ice cream
  Sweetened whipped cream
  Chocolate curls, for garnish (see Note)

1. Cut ginger in thin strips about 1 inch long. Place ginger strips, ginger syrup, and crème de cacao in a small bowl. Stir gently to thoroughly com-

bine all ingredients. Cover and let stand at room temperature to blend flavors (1 to 4 hours).

2. To serve, place 2 scoops of ice cream in each of 4 chilled individual dessert dishes. Spoon ginger sauce evenly over the ice cream. Dollop whipped cream (or pipe it from a pastry bag, using a star tip) around the ice cream.

3. Garnish with chocolate curls and serve at once.

Serves 4.

Note It is easiest to produce chocolate curls from a 4-ounce or larger bar of chocolate (at room temperature). Scrape the long side of the bar with a potato peeler. When chocolate is just the right temperature, this will produce nice curls. If chocolate is too cold, you will end up with short shavings or shredded chocolate.

This inviting three-course Danish menu is perfect for spring, when both asparagus—puréed in the creamy first-course soup—and salmon are in season. An enticing butter (made with orange and lemon peel and fresh mint) flavors salmon, green beans, and potatoes.

CREAM OF FILBERT SOUP

If you love the flavor of toasted nuts, this creamy beige soup is for you.

1½ cups filberts
¼ cup butter or margarine
1 leek, thinly sliced (use pale green part of top only)
1 stalk celery, thinly sliced
¼ cup thinly sliced carrot
1 small clove garlic, minced or pressed
Half a bay leaf
1 tablespoon flour
½ teaspoon salt
Pinch each ground nutmeg and white pepper
3½ cups Rich Chicken Broth (see page 8) or 2 cans (14½ oz each) chicken broth
1½ cups half-and-half
2 tablespoons brandy

1. Spread filberts in a large, shallow pan and bake in a 350° F oven until lightly browned (8 to 10 minutes). Let stand until cool enough to handle; with fingers, rub off as much of the skins as possible. Discard skins.

2. In a 3-quart saucepan over medium heat, melt butter. Add leek, celery, carrot, and garlic; cook, stirring often, until vegetables are soft but not browned. Mix in bay leaf and filberts, then flour, salt, nutmeg, and pepper. Stir until well combined and bubbling.

3. Gradually blend in broth. Cook, stirring often, until mixture boils. Reduce heat, cover, and simmer for 20 minutes.

4. Remove and discard bay leaf. Whirl filbert mixture, about half at a time, in blender or food processor until smooth. Return to pan and blend in half-and-half. Cook, stirring often, until steaming hot. *Do not boil.* Taste, and add salt if needed.

5. Stir in brandy and serve at once.

Makes about 7 cups. 6 servings.

FRENCH ALPINE SOUP

A veritable garden of vegetables—cauliflower, Swiss chard, carrot, celery, and onion—blends smoothly in this creamy, light-green soup.

3 tablespoons butter or margarine
1 medium onion, chopped
1 stalk celery, chopped
¼ cup thinly sliced carrot
3 cups cauliflowerets
2 cups lightly packed, coarsely chopped Swiss chard leaves (discard stems)
⅛ teaspoon white pepper
¼ teaspoon dried marjoram
Pinch cayenne pepper
3½ cups Rich Chicken Broth (see page 8) or 2 cans (14½ oz each) chicken broth
1 cup half-and-half
Salt (optional)

1. In a 3-quart saucepan over medium heat, melt butter. Add onion, celery, and carrot. Cook; stir occasionally, until soft but not browned. Mix in cauliflower, chard, pepper, marjoram, and cayenne. Add broth.

2. Bring to a boil, reduce heat, cover, and simmer until cauliflower is very tender (10 to 12 minutes).

3. Whirl mixture in blender or food processor until smooth.

4. Return to cooking pan, add half-and-half, and reheat to serving temperature. *Do not boil.* Taste, and add salt if needed. Serve hot.

Makes about 7 cups. 6 servings.

CHEDDAR-CAULIFLOWER SOUP

Creamy cauliflower soup gilded with a touch of Cheddar cheese makes a sturdy lunch or supper with bacon, lettuce, and tomato sandwiches.

1 cauliflower (1¼ to 1½ lbs)
1 small onion, thinly sliced
½ teaspoon dried chervil or parsley
1¾ cups Rich Chicken Broth (see page 8) or 1 can (14½ oz) chicken broth
2 tablespoons butter or margarine
1 tablespoon flour
¾ teaspoon salt
Pinch each ground nutmeg and white pepper
2 cups half-and-half
¼ pound sharp Cheddar cheese, shredded (1 cup)

1. Cut out and discard cauliflower core, remove and discard coarse outer leaves, and separate cauliflower into small flowerets. (You should have about 4 cups.)

2. In a 3-quart saucepan combine cauliflower, onion, chervil, and broth. Bring to a boil, cover, reduce heat, and simmer until cauliflower is tender (10 to 12 minutes). Set aside about a third of the cauliflower.

3. In a blender or food processor, whirl or process remaining cauliflower until smooth.

4. In a 3- to 4-quart saucepan over medium heat, melt butter. Stir in flour, salt, nutmeg, and pepper and cook, stirring, until bubbly. Remove from heat and gradually blend in half-and-half. Return to heat and cook, stirring constantly, until mixture boils. Blend in cauliflower purée and ¾ cup of the cheese. Heat, stirring often, until soup is steaming and cheese melts.

5. Add reserved cauliflower and cook just until heated through (2 to 3 minutes). Serve sprinkled with remaining ¼ cup cheese.

Makes about 6 cups. 5 or 6 servings.

LEEK AND POTATO SOUP

Leeks are one of the aristocrats of the onion family, with a flavor that is earthy yet suave. In concert with potatoes, they lend these qualities to a classic French soup.

> 6 medium leeks (2½ to 3 lbs)
> ¼ cup butter or margarine
> ⅛ teaspoon white pepper
> ¼ cup chopped fresh parsley
> 2 medium-sized smooth-skinned potatoes (about 1 lb), peeled and diced
> 3½ cups Rich Chicken Broth (see page 8) or 2 cans (14½ oz each) chicken broth
> ½ cup half-and-half
> Salt (optional)

1. Cut off root ends of leeks; remove and discard coarse outer leaves. Cut off and discard green tops so that leeks are about 9 inches long. Split lengthwise, from leafy end, cutting to within about 1 inch of root end. Soak in cold water for several minutes; then separate leaves under running water to rinse away any clinging grit; drain. Slice about ¼ inch thick.

2. In a 3-quart saucepan over medium heat, melt butter. Add leeks and cook, stirring often, until soft but not browned. Mix in pepper, parsley, potatoes, and broth. Bring to a boil, cover, reduce heat slightly, and boil gently until potatoes are very tender (25 to 30 minutes).

3. Purée mixture, about half at a time, in a blender or food processor until smooth. Return to cooking pan and stir in half-and-half. Taste, and add salt if needed. Reheat slowly to serving temperature, stirring often. *Do not boil.* Serve hot.

Makes about 7 cups, 6 servings.

BERNESE POTATO SOUP

From Switzerland's capital city comes this velvety potato soup with cheese, good as a starter or as a meal in itself with a crusty loaf and a green salad.

> ¼ cup butter or margarine
> 1 medium onion, chopped
> 1 small carrot, chopped
> 1 stalk celery, with leaves, chopped
> 1 clove garlic, minced or pressed
> ¼ teaspoon each white pepper and dried marjoram
> Pinch ground nutmeg
> 4 medium-sized smooth-skinned potatoes (about 1½ lbs), peeled and diced
> 3½ cups Rich Chicken Broth (see page 8) or 2 cans (14½ oz each) chicken broth
> 1 cup milk
> ¼ pound Swiss cheese, shredded (1 cup)
> Salt (optional)

1. In a 3- to 4-quart saucepan over medium heat, melt butter. Add onion, carrot, celery, and garlic and cook, stirring often, until soft but not browned. Mix in pepper, marjoram, nutmeg, potatoes, and broth. Bring to a boil, cover, reduce heat slightly, and boil gently until potatoes are very tender (25 to 30 minutes).

2. Purée soup, about half at a time, in a blender or food processor until smooth. Return to cooking pan.

3. Gradually blend in milk and reheat until steaming hot. *Do not boil.* Stir in cheese, about ¼ cup at a time, until it is smoothly melted into soup. Taste, and add salt if needed. Serve immediately.

Makes about 8 cups, 6 to 8 servings.

TIPS FOR FREEZING CHEESE

The freezer is a great place to store leftover bits of cheese. Cheeses that freeze well are the semihard and hard cheeses, such as Parmesan, Cheddar, Havarti, Muenster, Gruyère, Swiss, Gouda, Edam, Monterey jack, mozzarella, and the blue-veined cheeses. You can also freeze soft cheeses such as Camembert, Brie, and cream cheese.

Semihard and hard cheese can be frozen sliced, grated, or cut into blocks of convenient size. Frozen hard cheeses may be grated and then refrozen. Wrap blocks of cheese in freezer material; separate slices with a double thickness of waxed or freezer paper. Store grated cheese in plastic freezer bags or containers. Hard or semihard cheeses may become crumbly when thawed, but their flavor will not change. They are perfect to use when the recipe calls for grated cheese or when the cheese is to be melted.

Soft cheeses should be frozen when they have reached the desired degree of ripeness; wrap in freezer material. Overwrap prewrapped bricks of cream cheese before freezing.

Always thaw cheese in the refrigerator; thawing at room temperature causes cheese to crumble.

Alehouse Cheese Soup

Greens and Apple Salad

Whole Wheat Bread

Butter

Grapes

Plump Ginger Cookies

Tea

Cheese and apples are favorite flavor partners. For this lunch, the cheese is in the golden soup, and the apples accent the accompanying salad of mixed romaine and red leaf lettuce. If you're still hungry, you can munch on the Plump Ginger Cookies filled with currant jelly.

ALEHOUSE CHEESE SOUP

3 tablespoons butter or margarine
1 medium onion, chopped
2 stalks celery, thinly sliced
2 medium carrots, shredded
1 bottle or can (12 oz) dark beer
1¾ cups Rich Chicken Broth (see page 8) or 1 can (14½ oz) chicken broth
1 cup half-and-half
⅛ teaspoon ground nutmeg
¾ pound sharp Cheddar cheese, shredded (3 cups)
Salt and cayenne pepper

1. In a 3-quart saucepan over medium heat, melt butter. Add onion, celery, and carrots and cook, stirring often, until onion is soft but not browned. Add beer and chicken broth. Bring to a boil, cover, reduce heat, and simmer until vegetables are very tender (about 20 minutes).

2. Transfer mixture to a blender or food processor; whirl or process until smooth. Return to pan and add half-and-half and nutmeg. Heat over medium-low heat, stirring occasionally, until soup is steaming.

3. Add cheese, about 2 tablespoons at a time, whisking after each addition until cheese melts. *Do not let soup boil.* Season to taste with salt and cayenne. Serve at once.

Makes about 7 cups, 4 to 6 servings.

GREENS AND APPLE SALAD

4 cups each *torn romaine and red leaf lettuce*
2 small tart green apples, cored and thinly sliced (unpeeled)
⅓ cup coarsely chopped smoke-flavored almonds

Creamy Tarragon Dressing

1 egg yolk
1 tablespoon tarragon wine vinegar
1½ teaspoons Dijon mustard
⅛ teaspoon dried tarragon
Pinch white pepper
1 shallot, finely chopped
⅓ cup salad oil

1. In a large bowl combine greens and apples.

2. Prepare Creamy Tarragon Dressing; pour over salad and mix lightly.

3. Sprinkle with almonds and serve.

Serves 6.

Creamy Tarragon Dressing In a medium bowl mix egg yolk, vinegar, mustard, tarragon, pepper, and shallot. Using a whisk or fork, slowly and gradually beat in oil until dressing is thick and creamy.

Makes about ½ cup.

PLUMP GINGER COOKIES

¾ cup butter or margarine, softened
1 cup firmly packed brown sugar
1 egg
¼ cup light molasses
2¼ cups flour
½ cup ground walnuts
1¾ teaspoons baking soda
⅛ teaspoon salt
1 teaspoon each *ground ginger and cinnamon*
½ teaspoon ground cloves
Granulated sugar
3 to 4 tablespoons red currant jelly

1. Preheat oven to 350° F. In a large bowl cream butter and brown sugar until light and fluffy. Beat in egg, then molasses.

2. In a medium bowl stir together flour, walnuts, baking soda, salt, ginger, cinnamon, and cloves.

3. Gradually add flour mixture to butter mixture, mixing until well blended. Drop batter by heaping tablespoons into granulated sugar in a bowl. Roll each to form a ball, coating evenly with sugar. Place well apart on ungreased baking sheets.

4. With your finger or a small spoon, make a small, deep depression in center of each cookie; fill with currant jelly, using a rounded ¼ teaspoon for each.

5. Bake cookies until browned (15 to 18 minutes).

Makes 24 to 30 cookies.

Reminiscent of a Welsh rarebit, Alehouse Cheese Soup is tangy with Cheddar cheese and beer. It makes a perfect winter lunch when served with a crisp apple salad.

Peas cook with tender lettuce and piquant seasonings to make this creamy Curried Pea Soup, which can be enjoyed either hot or cold. Lemon zest makes an appropriate garnish.

TWO-WAY SOUPS: SERVE HOT OR CHILLED

Some soups are as delicious cold as they are hot. That means you can enjoy them regardless of the weather outdoors—steaming soup when it's gray and blustery, chilled soup to refresh you on a muggy day.

CURRIED PEA SOUP

When fresh peas are in season, it's worth the effort of shelling them for this piquantly seasoned soup. Otherwise, use about 2½ cups of frozen peas. When the soup is served hot, the curry flavor is assertive; chilled, it will taste more lemony. A dollop of yogurt is a nice finishing touch if you are serving the soup cold.

    2 pounds fresh peas in shells
    ¼ cup butter or margarine
    2 tablespoons salad oil
    2 medium onions, finely
       chopped
    1 large clove garlic, minced
       or pressed
    2 tablespoons curry powder
    1 teaspoon ground turmeric
    2 tablespoons flour
    1 small head butter or Boston
       lettuce, shredded (about
       4 cups, lightly packed)
       Grated rind and juice of
       1 lemon
    2 teaspoons sugar
    4 cups Rich Chicken Broth
       (see page 8) or canned
       chicken broth
    1 cup half-and-half
       Salt (optional)

1. Shell peas. (You should have about 2½ cups.) Reserve about 2 tablespoons small peas to use as garnish.

2. In a 3½- to 4-quart saucepan over medium heat, melt butter with oil. Add onion and garlic and cook, stirring often, until soft but not browned. Blend in curry powder and turmeric, then flour. Add shredded lettuce, lemon rind and juice, sugar, and peas, except for the reserved 2 tablespoons. Remove from heat and gradually blend in broth.

3. Bring to a boil, stirring, over medium heat; then cover, reduce heat, and simmer until peas are just tender (8 to 10 minutes). Blend in half-and-half. Taste, and add salt if needed.

4. Transfer mixture, about a third at a time, to food processor or blender and process or whirl until smooth.

5. *To serve cold,* cover and refrigerate until thoroughly chilled. *To serve hot,* return to cooking pan and heat, stirring often, until steaming hot. Serve garnished with reserved uncooked peas.

Makes about 9 cups, 6 to 8 servings.

MUSSEL SOUP BILLY-BI

Some trace the name of this recipe to a customer at a Deauville restaurant for whom this soup was created.

- 2 quarts (about 3 lbs) uncooked mussels in shells
- 2 tablespoons butter
- ¼ teaspoon paprika
- 4 shallots, finely chopped
- 3 sprigs parsley
- ¼ teaspoon whole white peppercorns
- 1 cup dry white wine
- 1½ to 2 cups Fish Broth (see page 11) or Rich Chicken Broth (see page 8) or 1 can (14½ oz) chicken broth
- 2 cups whipping cream
  Salt (optional)
  Italian (flat-leaf) parsley, for garnish

1. Discard any mussels that have opened. Scrape off barnacles, scrub mussels with a stiff brush under running water; drain.

2. In a 4- to 5-quart kettle over medium heat, melt butter. Add paprika and shallots and cook, stirring, until soft but not browned. Add mussels in shells, parsley, peppercorns, and wine. Bring to a boil, cover, reduce heat, and simmer until mussels open (6 to 8 minutes). Discard any mussels that remain closed.

3. Remove mussels from liquid. Strain liquid through a dampened cloth and measure it. Add Fish Broth to make 4 cups. Return liquid to kettle (rinsed to remove any sand).

4. Remove mussels from shells, discarding shells. Pinch out and discard any "beards" from the mussels.

5. To liquid add cream. Bring to a boil over high heat, reduce heat slightly, and boil until soup is reduced by about a fourth. Lower heat to medium. Taste, and add salt if needed. Add mussels and cook just until heated through.

6. Serve hot or chilled, garnished with parsley.

Makes 6 to 7 cups. 4 to 6 servings.

SHERRIED ARTICHOKE SOUP

When you offer this soup cold, at the very last moment pour about a tablespoon of whipping cream into the center of each serving (without stirring) to accent the subtle flavor of the artichoke.

- 2 tablespoons butter or margarine
- 1 medium onion, finely chopped
- 1 small clove garlic, minced or pressed
- 2 tablespoons flour
  Pinch ground nutmeg
- 1¾ cups Rich Chicken Broth (see page 8) or 1 can (14½ oz) chicken broth
- 1 package (9 oz) frozen artichoke hearts, thawed
- 2 tablespoons chopped parsley
- 1 cup half-and-half
  Salt and white pepper
- 3 tablespoons dry sherry
  Snipped fresh chives

1. In a 2- to 3-quart saucepan over medium heat, melt butter. Add onion and cook until soft. Stir in garlic, then flour and nutmeg. Cook, stirring, until mixture bubbles. Remove from heat; gradually blend in broth.

2. Add artichoke hearts and parsley to broth mixture. Cook over medium heat, stirring occasionally, until hearts are tender (6 to 8 minutes). Remove 3 or 4 of the artichoke hearts; chop and reserve them.

3. Purée the remaining artichoke mixture in a blender or food processor until smooth. Return purée to cooking pan; blend in half-and-half and reserved chopped artichokes. Season to taste with salt and pepper.

4. Cook over medium heat, stirring often, until steaming hot. Mix in sherry. Serve hot. Or cool slightly; then cover, refrigerate, and serve cold. Sprinkle chives on top.

Makes about 6 cups. 4 servings.

CREAM OF FRESH TOMATO SOUP

Fresh, ripe tomatoes make all the difference in the flavor of this orange-spiked cream soup.

- 2 pounds (about 4 large) tomatoes, peeled, seeded, and chopped
- 2 large onions, chopped
- 2 large carrots, sliced
- 2 tablespoons sugar
  Half a bay leaf
- ¾ teaspoon salt
- ⅛ teaspoon white pepper
  A 3-inch strip lemon rind
- 4 cups Rich Chicken Broth (see page 8) or canned chicken broth
- 2 tablespoons each butter or margarine, softened, and flour
- 1⅓ cups half-and-half
  Thinly shredded rind of 2 oranges, for garnish

1. In a 4- to 5-quart kettle, combine tomatoes, onions, carrots, sugar, bay leaf, salt, pepper, lemon rind, and chicken broth. Bring to a boil over moderately high heat, cover, reduce heat, and simmer for 30 minutes. Remove and discard bay leaf and lemon rind.

2. In a small bowl mix butter and flour until smooth; set aside.

3. Transfer tomato mixture, a fourth to a third at a time, to a food processor or blender and process or whirl until smooth. Return to kettle over medium heat. Stir in butter mixture, about a fourth at a time, mixing until soup thickens and boils.

4. Remove soup from heat; add half-and-half and stir to blend. Return soup to heat and cook, stirring occasionally, until steaming hot. *Do not boil.* Taste and add salt if needed. To serve cold, remove from heat after thickening, blend in half-and-half, and refrigerate until chilled.

5. Serve sprinkled with orange rind.

Makes 8 to 10 cups. 6 to 8 servings.

CHILLED SOUPS FOR HOT WEATHER

When the temperature soars, most people prefer to cool off with cold food and drink. Here are some cold soups for just such times. Two need no cooking at all, and the others can be made quickly.

GAZPACHO, UXMAL STYLE

Replete with crisp vegetables, this soup can be kept in the refrigerator for up to three days.

> 1 large can (28 oz) whole tomatoes
> 1 tablespoon red wine vinegar
> 3 tablespoons olive oil
> 1 cup tomato juice
> 1 clove garlic, minced or pressed
> 1 teaspoon salt
> ½ teaspoon each sugar and dried oregano
> 1 stalk celery, finely chopped
> 1 small fresh hot green chile, seeded and finely chopped or ⅛ teaspoon cayenne pepper
> ½ cup peeled, seeded, and chopped cucumber
> ¼ cup each finely chopped mild red onion and seeded green bell pepper
> ¼ cup sliced pimiento-stuffed green olives
> 1 avocado, peeled, seeded, and diced
> Lime wedges, Garlic Croutons (see page 76), sour cream, crumbled crisp bacon, and cilantro sprigs, as condiments

1. Reserving 2 whole tomatoes, purée remainder and liquid with vinegar, olive oil, tomato juice, garlic, salt, sugar, and oregano.

2. Pour purée into a large bowl. Add finely chopped reserved tomatoes, celery, green chile, cucumber, onion, bell pepper, and olives. Cover and chill at least 8 hours or up to 3 days.

3. Just before serving, mix in avocado. Serve cold, passing small bowls of condiments to add at table to taste.

Makes about 7 cups, 6 to 8 servings.

VICHYSSOISE

The French name leads some to think that this classic originated in France, but it is thought to have been created in the kitchen of a New York hotel.

> 5 medium leeks (2 to 2½ lbs)
> 2 tablespoons butter
> 1 small onion, finely chopped
> 3 medium smooth-skinned potatoes (1 to 1¼ lbs), peeled and diced
> 2 teaspoons salt
> ⅛ teaspoon white pepper
> 4 cups boiling water
> 1 cup milk
> 2 cups half-and-half
> 1 cup cold whipping cream
> Fresh chives, for garnish

1. Cut off root ends and tops of leeks. Clean, drain, and slice them about ¼ inch thick.

2. In a 3- to 4-quart saucepan over medium heat, melt butter. Add leeks and onion and cook, stirring often, until soft but not browned. Mix in potatoes, salt, pepper, and the boiling water. Bring to a boil, cover, reduce heat slightly, and cook until potatoes are very tender (25 to 30 minutes).

3. Purée mixture, about half at a time, in a blender or food processor until smooth. Return to cooking pan. Blend in milk and half-and-half. Stir over medium heat until steaming hot. Strain into a large bowl. Cover and refrigerate 3 to 5 hours or overnight.

4. Using a whisk, blend in cream. Taste, and add salt if needed.

5. Serve sprinkled with chives.

Makes 9 or 10 cups, 8 to 10 servings.

FROSTY WATERCRESS SOUP

This cold soup makes a refreshing summer lunch when served with plump croissant sandwiches.

> 2 bunches (about 12 oz) watercress
> 2 tablespoons butter or margarine
> 1 medium onion, chopped
> 1 shallot, chopped
> 1 bunch (about 6) green onions, sliced (use part of tops)
> 2 tablespoons flour
> ¼ teaspoon salt
> ⅛ teaspoon white pepper
> 3½ cups Rich Chicken Broth (see page 8) or 2 cans (14½ oz each) chicken broth
> 1 cup peas (fresh or frozen)
> 1 cup whipping cream
> Additional whipping cream and freshly ground white pepper, for garnish

1. Rinse watercress and drain well. Remove and discard coarse stems.

2. In a 3-quart saucepan over medium heat, melt butter. Add onion, shallot, and green onions and cook, stirring occasionally, until soft but not browned. Blend in flour, salt, and pepper, stirring until bubbly. Remove from heat and gradually blend in chicken broth. Bring to a boil, cover, reduce heat, and simmer for 15 minutes. Mix in peas and simmer, covered, for 3 minutes. Then stir in watercress, reserving 12 sprigs for garnish. Cover, remove from heat, and let stand for 5 minutes.

3. Purée watercress mixture, about half at a time, in a blender or food processor until smooth. Transfer to a glass bowl. Blend in whipping cream. Taste, and add salt, if needed.

4. Cover and refrigerate 3 to 5 hours or overnight. Top each serving with about 2 tablespoons whipping cream, a watercress sprig, and ground pepper.

Makes about 6½ cups, 6 servings.

GUADALAJARA AVOCADO SOUP

To preserve the fresh green color, prepare this soup no more than three hours before serving.

- 3 large soft-ripe avocados
- 4 green onions, thinly sliced (use part of tops)
- 1¾ cups Rich Chicken Broth (see page 8) or 1 can (14½ oz) chicken broth
- 2 tablespoons lime or lemon juice
- ½ teaspoon each salt and ground cumin
  Pinch cayenne pepper
- 2 tablespoons tequila
- 2 cups half-and-half
  Thin lime slices, for garnish

1. Peel and pit avocados; dice coarsely. (You should have about 4 cups.) Place in blender or food processor with green onions, broth, lime juice, salt, cumin, and cayenne. Whirl or process until very smooth.

2. Pour into a large glass bowl and blend in tequila, then half-and-half. Cover and refrigerate until thoroughly chilled (2 to 3 hours). Stir well; garnish with a lime slice.

Makes about 5½ cups, 6 servings.

CREAMY PINK BORSCHT

Served with black bread and butter, this fresh beet soup is a handsome beginning for a warm-weather meal.

- 3 medium beets (1½ to 2 lbs)
- 2 tablespoons butter
- 1 small onion, chopped
- 2 teaspoons brown sugar
- ¼ teaspoon salt
  Pinch each ground cloves and white pepper
- 3 cups Rich Chicken Broth (see page 8) or canned chicken broth
- 1 cup sour cream
- 1 tablespoon lemon juice
  Additional sour cream and fresh chives or dill, for garnish

1. Cut off all but about 1 inch of beet tops. Scrub beets well. Place in a large pan with salted water to cover.

Bring to a boil, cover, reduce heat, and cook until beets are tender (30 to 35 minutes). Cool, peel, and dice cooked beets.

2. In a 2½- to 3-quart saucepan over medium heat, melt butter. Add onion and cook until soft but not browned. Mix in brown sugar, salt, cloves, pepper, and diced beets. Add broth, bring to a boil, cover, reduce heat, and simmer for 20 minutes.

3. Purée mixture, about half at a time, with sour cream in a blender or food processor. Pour into a glass bowl; blend in lemon juice. Taste, and add salt if needed. Cover and refrigerate 3 to 5 hours or overnight.

4. Top with sour cream and chives.

Makes about 6 cups, 6 servings.

Feathery sprigs of fresh dill or snippets of chives accent a classic cold soup, Creamy Pink Borscht. Serve it with thinly sliced black bread and butter as a first course.

FRUIT SOUPS

It's said that a resourceful cook can make a good soup from anything. If you have never tried a fruit soup, consider serving one as a breakfast main dish—or for dessert.

A fruit soup is something like a sparkly, lightly cooked fruit compote. You can serve it hot or cold.

These fruit soup recipes follow the seasons: Rhubarb Soup With White Wine for spring, Raspberry-Peach Soup and Blueberry-Orange Soup for summer and early autumn, and Winter Fruit Soup with mixed dried fruits for the months in between.

RHUBARB SOUP WITH WHITE WINE

    4 cups diced rhubarb
       (1 to 1¼ lbs)
    1 cup water
    ¾ cup sugar
    1 cinnamon stick (2 in.)
    1 tablespoon cornstarch, mixed
       with 2 tablespoons water
    ½ cup dry white wine
       Few drops red food coloring
       (optional)
       Toasted sliced almonds,
       for garnish

1. In a 3-quart pan combine rhubarb, the water, sugar, and cinnamon stick. Bring to a boil over high heat; then reduce heat and simmer, uncovered, for 15 minutes.

2. Blend in cornstarch mixture and bring to a boil again over high heat, stirring until thickened and clear.

3. Remove from heat and blend in wine. If not pink enough, blend in a drop or two of food coloring.

4. Serve warm. Or cool slightly; then cover and refrigerate until thoroughly chilled (2 to 3 hours or overnight). Sprinkle almonds over each serving.

Makes about 3 cups, 4 to 6 servings.

RASPBERRY-PEACH SOUP

    ¾ cup each *water and sugar*
    1 *large peach, peeled and
       thinly sliced*
    2 *baskets (about 1½ cups
       each) raspberries*
    1 *tablespoon cornstarch, mixed
       with 2 tablespoons water*
    2 *teaspoons lemon juice*
    1 *tablespoon framboise or
       kirsch (clear fruit brandy)*
       Whipped cream

1. In a 2- to 3-quart saucepan, combine the water and sugar. Bring to a boil over high heat, stirring until sugar dissolves. Add peach and boil gently for 2 minutes. Add raspberries and bring to a boil again; boil for 1 minute.

2. Blend in cornstarch mixture; bring again to a boil, stirring until thickened and clear.

3. Remove from heat and stir in lemon juice and framboise. Serve hot. Or cool slightly; then cover and refrigerate until cold (2 to 3 hours or overnight). Spoon a dollop of whipped cream over each serving.

Makes about 3½ cups, 4 to 6 servings.

BLUEBERRY-ORANGE SOUP

    1 *orange*
    ⅔ *cup each water and sugar*
    3 *cups blueberries*
    ⅛ *teaspoon grated nutmeg*
    1 *tablespoon cornstarch, mixed
       with 2 tablespoons water*
    2 *teaspoons lemon juice*
       Whipping cream

1. Grate 2 teaspoons orange rind and reserve it. Squeeze juice from orange; strain out seeds if necessary.

2. In a 2- to 3-quart saucepan, combine orange juice, the water, and sugar. Bring to a boil over high heat, stirring until sugar dissolves. Add blueberries and bring again to a boil; boil for 1 minute. Blend in reserved orange rind and nutmeg; then add cornstarch mixture. Bring to a boil again, stirring until the soup is thickened and clear.

3. Remove from heat and stir in lemon juice. Serve hot. Or cool slightly; then cover and refrigerate until cold (2 to 3 hours or overnight). Accompany with cream to pour into each serving to taste, or whip cream until slightly thickened and spoon onto each serving.

Makes 3 cups, 4 servings.

WINTER FRUIT SOUP

    2 *packages (8 oz each) mixed
       dried fruits or about 3 cups
       mixed dried prunes, apricots,
       pears, peaches, and apples*
    ½ *cup sugar*
    2 *tablespoons quick-cooking
       tapioca*
    3 *cups water
       Grated rind and juice
       of 1 orange*
    1 *cinnamon stick (2 to 3 in.)
       Pinch salt
       Whipping cream*

1. Cut larger fruits, such as pears and peaches, into ½-inch-wide strips.

2. In a 2- to 3-quart saucepan, combine fruits, sugar, tapioca, the water, orange rind and juice, cinnamon stick, and salt. Bring to a boil over high heat, stirring until sugar dissolves.

3. Cover, reduce heat, and simmer until fruits are plump and tender but still retain their shapes (20 to 25 minutes).

4. Serve hot or at room temperature. Accompany with cream to pour into each serving to taste, or whip cream until slightly thickened and spoon onto each serving.

Makes about 5¾ cups, 6 servings.

You may find these tempting fruit soups somewhat too sweet to serve as a first course, but they make delicious breakfasts and tasty desserts.

Red-and-White Fish Chowder (see recipe on page 68) is a quick and satisfying full-meal soup. It contains red snapper, potatoes, red peppers, and cream.

Satisfying Full-Meal Soups

Into one big kettle go savory vegetables; juicy meats, chicken, or fish; pungent onions, garlic, and herbs; and often rice, dried beans, or pasta. What emerges hours later is a melting pot of flavors—a full-meal soup. Although you might assume that hearty soups are hours in the making, that isn't so. Many recipes in this chapter can be made in about an hour or less. Other soups, although they may take more time to cook, can be started one day, refrigerated, and then finished the next. Most soup enthusiasts agree that flavors improve when they can blend for a day or so.

SHORT-ORDER MEAT SOUPS

When you include ground meat or sausage, soup can be a speedy main dish for supper.

Tastefully chosen seasonings and some vegetables will give your quick-cooking soup plenty of flavor, especially if you start with a homemade stock (see pages 8–11) that you've tucked away in the freezer for just such an occasion.

These are all meat recipes; you can find other quick soups in the sections on soups with poultry (pages 60–67) and seafood (pages 68–71).

POLISH SAUSAGE AND CABBAGE SOUP

Here is a soup made with a garlicky sausage that lends its flavor to the delicious fresh vegetables around it. Serve the soup with milk or beer, dark bread with butter, and a warm fruit dessert such as an apple crisp.

- 2 tablespoons butter or margarine
- 1 stalk celery, thinly sliced
- 1 medium onion, slivered
- 1 medium-sized red or green bell pepper, seeded and chopped
- 1 medium potato (about ½ lb), diced
- 1 pound Polish sausage, cut in 1-inch pieces
- 1 bay leaf
- 3½ cups Rich Chicken Broth (see page 8) or 2 cans (14½ oz each) chicken broth
- ¼ cup chopped parsley
- 2 cups finely shredded cabbage
  Sour cream

1. In a 3- to 4-quart saucepan over medium heat, melt butter. Add celery, onion, and bell pepper and cook, stirring occasionally, until onion is soft but not browned.

2. Add potato, Polish sausage, bay leaf, and broth. Bring to a gentle boil, cover, reduce heat, and simmer until potato is tender (about 20 minutes).

3. Remove and discard bay leaf. Remove about 1 cup of the vegetables with a little of the broth to a blender or food processor. Whirl or process until smooth; then return to soup mixture in pan.

4. Add parsley and cabbage to soup. Stir often over medium heat until soup is steaming hot and cabbage is wilted and bright green (3 to 5 minutes).

5. Serve with sour cream to spoon onto each serving to taste.

Makes about 8 cups, 4 to 6 servings.

QUICK MEATBALL AND ZUCCHINI SOUP

Here is a soup that is a bargain in both time and money: The recipe makes four to six servings from just 1 pound of ground beef. Complete the menu with crusty rolls and a red jug wine, plus ice cream and chocolate chip cookies for dessert.

- 1 tablespoon olive oil or salad oil
- 1 large onion, slivered
- 1 clove garlic, minced or pressed
- 1 stalk celery, thinly sliced
- 8 baby carrots, sliced lengthwise
- 1 teaspoon dried basil
- ¼ teaspoon each dried thyme and oregano
- 1 large can (28 oz) tomatoes
- 1¾ cups Sturdy Beef Broth (see page 8) or 1 can (14½ oz) regular-strength beef broth
- 1 cup each dry red wine and water
- ½ cup bow tie pasta or other soup pasta
- 3 medium zucchini (about 1 lb)
  Salt (optional)
  Grated Parmesan cheese

Meatballs

- 1 egg, beaten
- ¼ cup each soft bread crumbs and grated Parmesan cheese
- ¾ teaspoon salt
- 1 clove garlic, minced or pressed
- 1 pound ground lean beef

1. Prepare Meatballs as directed. In a 4- to 6-quart Dutch oven, heat oil. Add meatballs and brown carefully over medium heat, removing them as they brown. To same pan add onion, garlic, celery, and carrot. Cook for 5 minutes, stirring occasionally.

2. Sprinkle with basil, thyme, and oregano; then add tomatoes (coarsely chopped) and their liquid, broth, wine, and the water. Return meatballs to pan. Bring soup to a boil, cover, reduce heat, and simmer for about 30 minutes.

3. Add pasta and cook, covered, at a gentle boil until it is nearly tender (12 to 15 minutes). Meanwhile, scrub zucchini and cut off ends. Cut into ⅜-inch-thick slices.

4. Add zucchini to soup and cook, uncovered, until zucchini is just tender (4 to 6 minutes). Taste, and add salt if needed.

5. Serve with Parmesan cheese to sprinkle over each serving to taste.

Makes about 13 cups, 4 to 6 servings.

Meatballs In a medium bowl mix together egg, bread crumbs, Parmesan cheese, salt, and garlic. Lightly mix in ground beef. Shape mixture into 1-inch meatballs.

Bow tie pasta and ground beef are cooked in Quick Meatball and Zucchini Soup—an economical one-dish meal that satisfies the heartiest of appetites.

Beef Soup au Pistou gets its name from the pungent paste of puréed basil and garlic that is stirred into the soup just before the tureen is brought to the table.

BEEF SOUP AU PISTOU

This traditional French soup is usually made without meat, but ground beef makes it even better. The word *pistou* refers to the pestolike paste of basil and garlic that flavors the soup. With it, serve a simple green salad, a baguette of French bread with sweet butter, and a light red wine. For dessert, spoon sweetened fresh strawberries over vanilla ice cream.

> 2 tablespoons olive oil
> 1½ pounds ground lean beef, crumbled
> 1 large onion, thinly slivered
> 1 clove garlic, minced or pressed
> 1 large can (28 oz) tomatoes
> 3½ cups Sturdy Beef Broth (see page 8) or 2 cans (14½ oz each) regular-strength beef broth
> 2 cups water
> 2 teaspoons salt
> ¼ teaspoon pepper
> 2 medium potatoes (about 1 lb), cut in ½-inch cubes
> 1 pound green beans, cut in 1-inch pieces
> ¼ pound vermicelli, broken in half
> ½ cup finely shredded Gruyère or Swiss cheese
> Additional shredded Gruyère or Swiss cheese

Pistou

> ¼ cup olive oil
> 3 cloves garlic, minced or pressed
> ½ cup lightly packed fresh basil leaves (or 2 tablespoons dried basil and ½ cup lightly packed chopped parsley)
> ¼ teaspoon each salt and sugar
> 1 tablespoon red wine vinegar

1. In a 5- to 6-quart kettle, heat oil. Add ground beef and cook over medium heat, stirring often. As meat begins to brown, stir in onion and continue cooking until onion is soft. Stir in garlic. Add tomatoes (coarsely chopped) and their liquid, broth, the water, salt, pepper, and potatoes.

2. Bring to a boil, cover, reduce heat, and simmer for 1 hour. Meanwhile, cook green beans, uncovered, in a large quantity of boiling salted water until they are tender-crisp (6 to 8 minutes). Drain and rinse immediately with cold water to stop cooking; drain and set aside.

3. Prepare Pistou. After soup has cooked for 1 hour, add vermicelli and boil gently, uncovered, stirring occasionally, until pasta is just tender (10 to 12 minutes). Add green beans and cook just until the beans are heated through.

4. Add the ½ cup Gruyère cheese, about a fourth at a time, stirring after each addition until cheese melts.

5. Place Pistou in a warm tureen, add soup, and stir until soup and Pistou are well blended. Serve at once with additional shredded cheese to add to each serving to taste.

Makes about 16 cups, 6 to 8 servings.

Pistou In blender or food processor combine olive oil, garlic, basil, salt, sugar, and vinegar. Whirl until smooth.

Makes about ⅓ cup.

EASY LAMB, SPINACH, AND GARBANZO SOUP

Fresh lemon accents a savory soup with North African flavors. Made with ground lamb, it is especially good with warm pocket bread, beer, and a citrus-flavored sherbet for dessert.

> 1 tablespoon olive oil or salad oil
> 1 pound ground lean lamb, crumbled
> 1 large onion, thinly slivered
> 1 stalk celery, finely chopped
> 2 cloves garlic, minced or pressed
> ½ teaspoon each salt and ground cumin
> ⅛ teaspoon ground allspice
> 1 can (15 oz) garbanzos (ceci beans or chick-peas)
> 1 can (15 oz) tomato purée
> 1¾ cups Rich Chicken Broth (see page 8) or 1 can (14½ oz) chicken broth
> 2 bunches (12 oz each) spinach
> 1 tablespoon grated lemon rind
> Plain yogurt or sour cream

1. In a 3- to 4-quart saucepan, heat oil over medium heat. Add lamb and cook, stirring often, until meat loses its pink color. Add onion and celery; cook, stirring often, until onion is soft but not browned. Mix in garlic, salt, cumin, and allspice.

2. Add garbanzos and their liquid, tomato purée, and broth. Bring to a boil, cover, reduce heat, and simmer for 30 minutes.

3. Meanwhile, wash spinach and drain well; discard stems. Slice leaves into about ½-inch-wide strips. (You should have about 8 cups.)

4. After soup has simmered for 30 minutes, add spinach and cook, uncovered, stirring often, until soup returns to a boil. Mix in lemon rind. Taste, and add salt if needed.

5. Top each serving with yogurt or sour cream.

Makes about 12 cups, 4 to 6 servings.

MEATY SOUPS

Here you will find those slowly cooked soups that begin with a hefty pot of meaty bones—beef, pork or ham, or lamb. Remember, you can make all these soups a day or more in advance. Reheat them just before serving, waiting until this final stage to add any bright green vegetables.

PETITE MARMITE

Here is another soup hearty with beef. This one is French in origin and has the distinction of being cooked in the oven. It takes its name from the deep earthenware casserole (*marmite*) in which it bakes.

If you wish to make the soup ahead of time, you can proceed through step 4. After baking for about 4 hours, cool the casserole, then refrigerate it. To serve, let it stand at room temperature for about an hour. Then proceed with step 5.

Either way, complement the soup's subtle spiciness by serving it with a velvety red wine.

Substitute Herbed Sourdough Thins (see page 75) for the Toasted Cheese Croutons, if you wish.

- 1 tablespoon each *butter or margarine and salad oil*
- 3½ to 4 pounds *beef shanks, sliced about 1 inch thick*
- 1 pound *chicken wings*
- ½ pound *chicken livers*
- 2 medium *onions, slivered*
- 2 cloves *garlic, minced or pressed*
- ½ teaspoon *dried thyme*
- 8 cups *hot water*
- 1 *bay leaf*
- 3 sprigs *parsley*
- ¼ teaspoon each *whole cloves, whole allspice, and black peppercorns*
- 3 or 4 *leeks*
- 2 small *turnips (about ½ lb), peeled and cut in sixths*
- 1 stalk *celery, thinly sliced*
- 3 medium *carrots, thinly sliced*
- 1 teaspoon *salt*

Toasted Cheese Croutons

- 2 tablespoons *butter or margarine*
- 1 tablespoon *olive oil*
- 1 small clove *garlic, minced or pressed*
- 1 baguette *(8 oz), sliced crosswise to make 24 thin slices*
- 1 cup thinly shredded *Gruyère or Swiss cheese*

1. Preheat oven to 350° F. In a large, heavy frying pan over medium heat, heat together butter and oil and brown beef shanks, 3 or 4 at a time. As they brown, transfer shanks to a deep 5- to 6-quart marmite. Brown chicken wings and add them to marmite. Then brown chicken livers; remove to a shallow bowl, cover, and refrigerate until step 5. In the same pan, cook onions, stirring often, until soft and lightly browned; mix in garlic and thyme. Add onion mixture to marmite. Add a little of the water to frying pan, stirring to loosen drippings; add mixture to marmite.

2. Place bay leaf, parsley, cloves, allspice, and peppercorns in a square cut from a double thickness of cheesecloth. Tie cloth to enclose seasonings securely; add to marmite.

3. Cut off root ends of leeks; then cut off green tops so that leeks are about 5 inches long. Remove coarse outer leaves. Rinse well to remove all grit between the leaves. Slice leeks about ¼ inch thick and add to marmite with turnips, celery, carrots, and salt. Add remaining hot water.

4. Cover marmite and place in oven. Bake, stirring once or twice, until beef is tender and broth is richly flavored (3½ to 4 hours).

5. Add browned chicken livers, return to oven. Bake about 45 minutes more.

6. With tongs, remove and discard seasonings in cheesecloth. Skim and discard surface fat, if necessary. Taste broth, and add salt if needed.

7. Serve soup in individual bowls with croutons either floating atop soup or on the side to eat as crackers.

Makes about 15 cups, 6 servings.

Toasted Cheese Croutons Preheat oven to 300° F. In a small pan over medium heat, melt butter; add oil and garlic. Place bread slices in a single layer on a baking sheet. Brush with the butter mixture. Bake until crisp and lightly browned (20 to 25 minutes). Sprinkle evenly with cheese. Place about 4 inches below broiler and broil until cheese melts and browns lightly (2 to 3 minutes). Serve croutons hot.
Makes 2 dozen croutons.

SUNDAY NIGHT VEGETABLE-BEEF SOUP

Make this soup into a meal with whole-grain crackers, milk, favorite cheeses, and fresh fruit for dessert.

- 2 tablespoons *butter or margarine*
- 3 to 3½ pounds *beef short ribs*
- 2 medium *onions, finely chopped*
- 2 stalks *celery, thinly sliced*
- 3 cloves *garlic, slivered*
- 1 red or green *bell pepper, seeded and chopped*
- 1 teaspoon *chili powder*
- 1 large can *(28 oz) tomatoes, coarsely chopped, and their liquid*
- 2 large *carrots, thinly sliced*
- 2 medium-sized *red potatoes (about 1 lb), scrubbed (unpeeled) and diced*
- 1 *bay leaf*
- 2 teaspoons *salt*
- ¼ teaspoon *pepper*
- ½ teaspoon *dried marjoram*
- 8 cups *water*
- ½ cup *alphabet pasta or other tiny soup pasta (pastina)*
- ½ cup *chopped parsley*

1. In a 6- to 8-quart kettle or Dutch oven over medium heat, melt butter and brown short ribs well on all sides. As you turn short ribs to brown last side, add onion, celery, garlic, and bell pepper around them, stirring occasionally until vegetables are limp. Sprinkle with chili powder.

2. Add tomatoes and liquid, carrots, potatoes, bay leaf, salt, pepper, marjoram, and water. Bring to a boil, cover, reduce heat, and simmer until meat is very tender (3 to 4 hours).

3. Remove and discard bay leaf. Remove short ribs; when cool, remove meat from bones. Cut meat into chunks and return it to soup; discard fat and bones. Cover and refrigerate soup for several hours or overnight.

4. To serve, skim and discard surface fat from soup. Bring to a boil over medium-high heat. Add pasta and boil gently, uncovered, until noodles are tender (10 to 12 minutes). Taste soup, and add salt if needed. Stir in parsley and serve at once.

Makes about 16 cups. 6 to 8 servings.

The bones are removed from the short ribs included in the nourishing Sunday Night Vegetable-Beef Soup so that you can concentrate on enjoying the flavor. Cook it on Saturday night, and pull it out of the refrigerator after an invigorating Sunday hike.

DRYING VEGETABLES

When the first colonists arrived in the New World, the natives were already using fire and sun to dry their food. In fact, the Indians are said to have taught the early settlers how to dry corn and grind it into meal.

Although dried vegetables can never take the place of just-picked ones, drying your garden surplus will provide you with the makings of hearty soups throughout the winter.

The key to drying food successfully is controlling temperature and air circulation. Warmth causes excess moisture in the food to evaporate; movement of air over the food carries the moisture away. (Home-dried vegetables retain only 5 to 20 percent of their original moisture.) If the temperature is too low, food will dry too slowly and may spoil. If the temperature is too high, food will cook, or the outside surface will harden, locking moisture inside that will cause the food to deteriorate eventually.

Some vegetables, notably asparagus, broccoli, and cauliflower, do not rehydrate well; they'll taste far better if preserved by freezing. Others—carrots and onions, for example—are available the year around and are therefore not worth drying. Vegetables that dry well include chile peppers, bell peppers, tomatoes, carrots, lentils, peas, shell beans, and sweet corn.

Prepare vegetables by washing them carefully in cold water and patting them dry. Cut into uniformly sized pieces so that they will dry at the same rate. Most vegetables need to be pretreated by blanching before drying to deactivate the enzymes that cause ripening and decay.

You can dry vegetables in a dehydrator, in an oven, or in the sun.

Dehydrators Using a dehydrator is by far the simplest method of drying because it involves fewer variables than sun- or oven-drying. Dehydrators perform best indoors, in a dry, well-ventilated room. Operating instructions vary from model to model, so consult your manual.

Ovens To use the oven, you must be able to maintain a low heat of 120° to 140° F. Heat should come only from the bottom of the oven. Spread vegetables directly on racks. Baking sheets are not recommended because they do not allow air to circulate around the food. Drying time will vary, according to the type of vegetable, from 8 to 18 hours.

Sun-Drying Sun-drying is the oldest method, and also takes the longest; 4 to 5 days of hot sun are needed to dry most foods. Spread vegetables on drying trays (a frame covered with nylon netting will do) and place on a platform in direct sunlight.

Storing Dried vegetables should generally have a brittle or tough-to-brittle consistency. As a precaution, sun-dried vegetables should be pasteurized before storing. Do this by sealing dried foods in plastic food storage bags and placing them in the freezer at 0° F for at least 2 days. Then package the vegetables in airtight containers and store in a cool, dry, dark place.

Using Dried Vegetables To use dried vegetables, the water removed during drying must be replaced by soaking, cooking, or a combination of the two. Depending on the kind and the thickness, dried vegetables can take anywhere from 20 minutes to 2 hours to rehydrate.

SPRINGTIME VEAL AND VEGETABLE SOUP

The meaty veal shanks known in Italian cooking as *osso buco* add real substance to the stock that unites this enticing soup. With fresh green vegetables added just before you serve it, the soup needs few accompaniments beyond a full-bodied white wine and a good loaf of French bread. Spread the bread with either butter or the veal bone marrow.

> 6 *leeks*
> 2 *tablespoons butter or margarine*
> 2 *medium onions, slivered*
> 2 *cloves garlic, minced or pressed*
> 3 *medium carrots, thinly sliced*
> 4 *medium-sized, smooth-skinned potatoes (1½ to 2 lbs), sliced about ¼ inch thick*
> 1 *ham hock (½ to ¾ lb)*
> 3 *to 4 pounds veal shanks, cut in about 2-inch slices*
> ½ *teaspoon dried savory*
> ¼ *teaspoon white pepper*
> 8 *cups water*
> ½ *pound asparagus*
> ⅓ *cup shelled fresh or frozen peas*
> *Salt (optional)*
> ¼ *cup chopped parsley*

1. Cut root ends from leeks; remove and discard coarse outer leaves. Cut off and discard green tops so that leeks are about 8 inches long. Split lengthwise, from leafy end, cutting to within about 1 inch of root end. Soak in cold water for several minutes, then separate leaves under running water to rinse away any clinging grit; drain. Slice about ¼ inch thick.

2. In a 6- to 8-quart kettle, melt butter and cook leeks and onions over medium heat, stirring often, until soft but not browned. Mix in garlic and carrots. Add potatoes, ham hock, veal shanks, savory, pepper, and the water. Bring slowly to a boil, cover, reduce heat, and simmer until veal and ham are very tender (about 2½ to 3 hours).

3. Meanwhile, snap off and discard fibrous ends of asparagus. Slice stalks diagonally about ½ inch thick, keeping tips separate. Set aside.

4. Remove ham hock from soup; when it is cool enough to handle, remove and discard bones and skin. Return meat to soup in chunks. Increase heat to moderate. Stir in asparagus slices and cook, uncovered, for 5 minutes. Then mix in asparagus tips and peas; cook, uncovered, just until asparagus is tender-crisp (about 3 minutes). Taste soup, and add salt if needed. Stir in parsley.

5. To serve, place a veal shank in each bowl; then spoon vegetables and broth over and around it.

Makes about 5 quarts, 8 to 10 servings.

Provide knives as well as spoons with this Springtime Veal and Vegetable Soup, so that people can pick out the tasty marrow from the veal shanks and spread it on French bread.

*A mixture of winter vegetables,
barley, and lamb goes into
Scotch Broth. The soup is best if it
is chilled, then skimmed of fat
before you finish cooking it.*

SCOTCH BROTH

Chunky lamb neck or shoulder makes this barley and vegetable soup a substantial repast. Plan to start a day in advance. Serve it with a crusty whole-grain bread and butter, and a light red wine if you wish.

½ cup pearl barley
2 tablespoons butter or margarine
3 pounds bone-in lamb neck, in large chunks
1 large onion, finely chopped
2 cloves garlic, minced or pressed
1 red or green bell pepper, seeded and chopped
2 medium carrots, chopped
1 small celery root (about ½ lb), peeled and finely chopped
1 bay leaf
1 teaspoon salt
¼ teaspoon each white pepper and dried thyme
  Pinch ground allspice
8 cups water
¼ cup chopped parsley

1. Place barley in a small bowl, cover with water, and let stand for 8 hours or overnight.

2. Meanwhile, in a 5½- to 6-quart kettle over medium heat, melt butter. Add lamb pieces, and brown, about half at a time, on all sides, removing lamb as it browns. To same kettle add onion and cook, stirring occasionally, until soft. Mix in garlic, bell pepper, carrots, and celery root. Return lamb to pot; then add bay leaf, salt, white pepper, thyme, allspice, and the 8 cups water. Bring to a boil, cover, reduce heat, and simmer until lamb is very tender (2½ to 3 hours).

3. Remove chunks of lamb from soup. Remove and discard bay leaf. When lamb is cool enough to handle, remove and discard bones and fat. Return meat to soup in large chunks. Cover and refrigerate for several hours or overnight.

4. Skim and discard fat from soup. Drain soaked barley and add it to the soup. Bring soup slowly to a boil, stirring occasionally; then cover, reduce heat, and boil gently until barley is tender (45 minutes to 1 hour).

5. Taste, and add salt if needed. Stir in parsley and serve at once.

Makes about 12 cups, 6 servings.

SPANISH BEAN AND SAUSAGE SOUP

Served with a basket of cherry tomatoes, French rolls with butter, and an unpretentious red wine, *caldo gallego* makes a satisfying meal. For dessert, dot fresh fruit—such as papaya, pineapple, or halved bananas—with butter and brown sugar; then broil until the tops are golden.

1 pound (about 2½ cups) dried small white beans, rinsed and drained
8 cups water
2 smoked ham hocks (about 1½ lbs)
1 large onion, finely chopped
2 stalks celery, with leaves, finely chopped
1 large clove garlic, minced or pressed
2 medium potatoes (about 1 lb), diced
2 small turnips (about ½ lb), peeled and diced
4 small chorizo sausages (about ¾ lb)
1 bunch spinach (about 12 oz)
  Salt (optional)
  Cilantro (Chinese parsley), for garnish

1. Place beans in a large bowl; add 2 teaspoons salt and 6 cups water.

Cover and let stand for at least 8 hours; drain, discarding soaking liquid. Or, to shorten the soaking period, place beans in a 3- to 4-quart pan with 8 cups water (*no salt*); bring to a boil; then boil briskly, uncovered, for 2 minutes. Remove from heat, cover, and let stand for about 1 hour. Drain and discard the soaking liquid.

2. In a 5- to 6-quart kettle, combine drained beans, the 8 cups water, ham hocks, onion, celery, garlic, potatoes, and turnips. Bring to a boil over medium heat. Cover, reduce heat, and boil gently until beans are very tender (3½ to 4 hours).

3. Meanwhile, remove and discard sausage casings and slice sausages ½ inch thick. In a medium frying pan over moderate heat, cook sausages in their own drippings, stirring often, until lightly browned. Remove sausages with a slotted spoon, drain on paper towels, and reserve.

4. Remove ham hocks from beans. When they are cool enough to handle, discard bones and skin; cut ham into large chunks and return to soup. Add prepared sausage; then cook, uncovered, stirring occasionally, for about 10 minutes.

5. Meanwhile, rinse and drain spinach. Remove and discard stems. Coarsely shred leaves; add to soup and cook, stirring, until spinach is just wilted and bright green. Taste, and add salt if needed.

6. Serve hot soup garnished with sprigs of cilantro.

Makes 12 to 14 cups, 6 to 8 servings.

Start off an Italian dinner with apéritifs and a buttery tuna spread on toast rounds. Conclude with fruit and Italian cheeses such as Taleggio and Parmesan.

ITALIAN SOUP SUPPER

Tuna Toasts

Apéritifs

Minestrone Milanese

Bread Sticks

Pears or Fresh Figs

Cheeses

Spiced Nut Cookies

Red Wine

Espresso Coffee

This minestrone is smoky with ham and thick with rice in the style of Milan. For wine, select a light Zinfandel or a Chianti.

Serve cheeses that go well with pears or figs, such as Taleggio (a creamy, Brie-like soft cheese), rich Fontina, and a nutty (not too dry) Parmesan. With coffee, enjoy the chewy cookies, known as quaresimali in Italy.

TUNA TOASTS

These crisp little herbed toast rounds are called *crostini* in Italy where they are a favorite first course. They are normally enjoyed with apéritifs such as Campari, Cynar, or vermouth.

The spread served with these toasts is usually a purée of savory chicken livers, but here it is a tuna mixture.

> 1 large can (12½ oz) oil-packed tuna, drained
> 1 cup butter or margarine
> ½ cup whipping cream
> 1 teaspoon Dijon mustard
> 1 small dried hot red chile, finely crushed
> ¼ teaspoon coarsely ground black pepper
> 2 tablespoons chopped capers
> ¼ cup chopped parsley
> ½ cup chopped pimiento-stuffed olives
> Salt (optional)
> Herbed Sourdough Thins (see page 75), thinly sliced French bread, or crackers

1. Place tuna in food processor. Cut butter in pieces and add to tuna with cream, mustard, chile, and pepper. Process until mixture is smooth.

2. Turn into a bowl and blend in capers, parsley, and ¼ cup of the olives. Taste, and add salt if needed. Spread in a crock or terrine. Cover and refrigerate until mixture is firm and flavors are well blended (2 to 3 hours or overnight).

3. Remove from refrigerator about 30 minutes before serving. Garnish with remaining chopped olives and serve with Herbed Sourdough Thins.

Makes about 3½ cups.

MINESTRONE MILANESE

- 1 cup dried cannellini or Great Northern beans, rinsed and drained
- 2 tablespoons olive oil
- 2½ to 3 pounds beef shanks, sliced ¾ to 1 inch thick
- 2 large onions, slivered
- 2 large carrots, chopped
- 2 stalks celery, thinly sliced
- 2 cloves garlic, minced or pressed
- ½ cup chopped parsley
- 1 smoked ham hock (about ¾ lb)
- 1 large can (28 oz) tomatoes
- 2 tablespoons dried basil
- 8 cups water
- 1 medium turnip, peeled and diced
- 2 cups chopped chard leaves
- ½ cup shelled fresh or frozen peas
- 1½ cups hot cooked rice
- 2 cups shredded cabbage
  Salt (optional)
  Grated Parmesan cheese

1. Place beans in a large bowl; add 1 teaspoon salt and 3 cups water. Cover and let stand for at least 8 hours; drain, discarding soaking liquid. Or, to shorten the soaking period, place beans in a 2- to 3-quart pan with 4 cups water (*no salt*); bring to a boil; then boil briskly, uncovered, for 2 minutes. Remove from heat, cover, and let stand for 1 hour. Drain, discarding soaking liquid.

2. In a 7- to 8-quart kettle, heat olive oil over medium heat. Add beef shanks and brown on all sides. As you turn shanks to brown last side, add onions; cook, stirring occasionally, until onions are limp.

3. Add carrots, celery, garlic, parsley, ham hock, tomatoes (coarsely chopped) along with their liquid, basil, drained soaked beans, and the 8 cups water. Bring to a boil, cover, reduce heat, and simmer until meats and beans are tender (3½ to 4 hours). Skim and discard surface fat if necessary.

4. Remove beef shanks and ham hock with a slotted spoon. When cool enough to handle, discard bones and skin. Return beef and ham in large chunks to soup. (At this point, soup may be covered and refrigerated until ready to reheat and serve; skim fat from surface before reheating.)

5. Add turnip to soup and boil gently, uncovered, for 10 minutes. Mix in chard and peas and cook for 3 minutes more. Blend in rice and cabbage and cook, stirring occasionally, just until cabbage is wilted and bright green (3 to 5 minutes). Taste, and add salt if needed.

6. Serve with Parmesan cheese to sprinkle over each serving.

Makes about 5½ quarts, 8 to 10 servings.

SPICED NUT COOKIES

- 2½ cups flour
- 1½ teaspoons baking powder
- 1 teaspoon ground cinnamon
- ½ teaspoon ground nutmeg
- ¼ teaspoon each *salt and ground allspice*
- ¼ cup butter or margarine, softened
- 1 cup sugar
- 1 teaspoon vanilla extract
- 3 eggs
- 1 cup each *unblanched whole filberts or almonds and coarsely chopped walnuts*
- ⅓ cup pine nuts
  Sugar, for sprinkling

1. In a medium bowl stir flour, baking powder, cinnamon, nutmeg, salt, and allspice to blend well.

2. In a large bowl beat butter with the 1 cup sugar until well combined. Blend in vanilla. Separate 1 of the eggs, reserving the white.

3. To butter mixture add the egg yolk, then the remaining whole eggs, one at a time, beating after each addition until smooth.

4. Gradually add flour mixture to butter mixture, mixing until smooth and well blended. Divide dough in half and wrap each portion in plastic wrap; refrigerate until firm (about 1 hour). Meanwhile, mix filberts, walnuts, and pine nuts.

5. Preheat oven to 350° F. On a lightly floured board or pastry cloth, roll out each portion of dough to an 8- by 12-inch rectangle. Sprinkle half of the nuts over each portion. Starting with a long side of each rectangle, roll dough to make a compact roll; pinch edge and ends to seal. Place, sealed side down, on a lightly greased baking sheet.

6. Beat the reserved egg white until slightly bubbly and brush generously over each roll. Sprinkle rolls lightly with sugar.

7. Bake until golden brown (35 to 40 minutes). Remove from oven and allow rolls to cool on baking sheet for about 5 minutes.

8. Transfer rolls to a board and, using a serrated knife, slice each loaf diagonally into ½-inch-thick slices. Lay slices flat on baking sheets and bake them again in 350° F oven until crisply toasted (15 to 20 minutes). Cool on racks.

Makes about 4 dozen cookies.

SWISS LENTIL, HAM, AND VEGETABLE SOUP

Lentils cook more quickly than other dried legumes and make an appealing soup with vegetables and ham hocks. Serve the soup with a crusty light rye bread and beer, then berries with cream for dessert.

- ¼ cup dried mushrooms
- 2 leeks
- 2 tablespoons butter or margarine
- 2 medium carrots, chopped
- 2 medium onions, slivered
- 1 stalk celery, thinly sliced
- 1 clove garlic, minced or pressed
- 10 cups water
- 1 pound (about 2½ cups) dried lentils, rinsed and drained
- 1 medium potato (about ½ lb), finely diced
- 1 large tomato, peeled and chopped
- 4 smoked ham hocks (2½ to 3 lbs)
- ¾ cup chopped parsley
- ¼ teaspoon white pepper
- 1 teaspoon mustard seed, crushed
- 1 bay leaf
  Salt (optional)
- 2 hard-cooked eggs, shredded

1. Place mushrooms in a small bowl and cover with hot water; let stand until soft (30 minutes to 1 hour).

2. Meanwhile, cut off root ends of leeks; remove and discard coarse outer leaves. Cut off and discard green tops so that leeks are about 9 inches long. Split lengthwise, from leafy end, cutting to within about 1 inch of root end. Soak in cold water for several minutes; then separate leaves under running water to rinse away any clinging grit; drain. Slice about ¼ inch thick.

3. In a 6- to 8-quart kettle over medium heat, melt butter. Add leeks, carrots, onions, celery, and garlic and cook, stirring often, until they are soft but not browned.

4. To vegetables add the water, lentils, potato, tomato, ham hocks, ½ cup of the parsley, the pepper, mustard seed, and bay leaf. Bring to a boil. Meanwhile, drain mushrooms and chop coarsely; add to lentil mixture. When it begins to boil, cover, reduce heat, and simmer until ham is very tender (3 to 3½ hours).

5. Remove and discard bay leaf. Remove ham hocks. Purée about 2 cups of the lentils and vegetables in blender or food processor; then return to soup. When ham hocks are cool enough to handle, discard bones and skin; return ham in large chunks to soup. Taste, and add salt if needed. Reheat if necessary.

6. Serve hot, garnishing each serving with hard-cooked egg and some of the remaining chopped parsley.

Makes about 14 cups, 6 servings.

RED BEANS, RIBS, AND HOT SAUSAGE POT

Hot Louisiana-style sausage lights the flavor fire of this hearty, chili-like soup. You can vary the quantity of sausage as indicated to make the soup hot or hotter, as you prefer. With the soup, munch on crisp soda crackers and drink ice-cold beer.

- 1½ cups dried small red beans, rinsed and drained
- 2 teaspoons salad oil
- 2 to 2½ pounds country-style spareribs
- 2 large onions, finely chopped
- 1 stalk celery, thinly sliced
- 1 medium carrot, shredded
- 2 cloves garlic, minced or pressed
- 1 green bell pepper, seeded and chopped
- 1 bay leaf
- ½ teaspoon dried oregano
- ¼ teaspoon pepper
- 6 cups water
- ¾ to 1 pound Louisiana hot sausages
- 1 can (1 lb) tomatoes
  Salt (optional)
- 2 to 3 tablespoons red wine vinegar

1. Place beans in a large bowl; add 1 teaspoon salt and 3 cups water. Cover and let stand for at least 8 hours; drain, discarding soaking liquid. Or, to shorten the soaking period, place beans in a 2- to 3-quart pan with 4 cups water (*no salt*); bring to a boil; then boil briskly, uncovered, for 2 minutes. Remove from heat, cover, and let stand for 1 hour. Drain, discarding soaking liquid.

2. In a 5½- to 6-quart kettle, heat oil over medium heat. Add spareribs and brown on all sides, removing ribs as they brown. (Do not crowd pan.) When all ribs are browned, add onions to same pan; cook, stirring often, until lightly browned. Mix in celery, carrot, garlic, bell pepper, bay leaf, oregano, and pepper.

3. Return browned ribs to pan. Add drained beans and the 6 cups water. Bring to a boil, cover, reduce heat, and simmer until meat is tender (about 3 hours). Remove spareribs from pan; when they are cool enough to handle, return meat to pot in large chunks, discarding bones and fat. (At this point, soup may be covered and refrigerated until the next day if you wish.) Skim off and discard surface fat from soup.

4. Remove casings from sausages; cut in 1-inch chunks. Add to soup with tomatoes (coarsely chopped) and their liquid. Return soup to medium heat and bring slowly to a boil; then cover, reduce heat, and simmer until beans are tender and soup is thick (about 1 hour). Taste, and add salt if needed. Season to taste with vinegar.

5. Serve hot.

Makes about 16 cups, 6 to 8 servings.

CRANBERRY BEAN MINESTRONE

If you shop in a neighborhood with an Italian heritage, you may have seen fresh cranberry beans in the markets in September and October. Sold in pods flecked with cranberry red, they need to be shelled before cooking. Though fresh, the beans still take half an hour or longer to cook.

This colorful soup takes advantage of the special character of these beans. If you can't find them, or when they are out of season, you can make the soup using 2 cups of different kinds of cooked dried red or white beans, or drained canned kidney or pinto beans.

Serve the soup with thick slices of Italian bread, red wine, and for dessert, fresh pineapple flavored with a little kirsch.

 1½ pounds fresh cranberry beans
 2 tablespoons olive oil
 1 pound mild Italian pork
   sausages
 1 large onion, finely chopped
 1 large carrot, cut lengthwise in
   quarters, then thinly sliced
 1 stalk celery, thinly sliced
 1 large clove garlic, minced
   or pressed
 1 red or green bell pepper,
   seeded and chopped
 ¼ cup chopped parsley
 1 teaspoon dried basil
 ½ teaspoon dried oregano
 ¼ teaspoon dried marjoram
 1 large can (about 30 oz)
   tomatoes packed in tomato
   sauce
 3½ cups Sturdy Beef Broth
   (see page 8) or 2 cans
   (14½ oz each) regular-
   strength beef broth
 ½ cup dry red wine
 ¼ cup tiny soup pasta (pastina)
 4 cups coarsely shredded fresh
   spinach leaves
   Salt (optional)
   Grated Parmesan cheese

1. Split bean pods and slip out beans as if shelling peas. (You should have about 2 cups beans.)

2. In a 5- to 6-quart Dutch oven, heat oil over medium heat. Remove casings from sausages and crumble meat into Dutch oven; cook sausage until lightly browned, stirring often. Mix in onion, carrot, and celery; cook, stirring often, until onion is soft. If drippings are excessive, spoon off and discard most of the fat.

3. Add shelled beans, garlic, bell pepper, parsley, herbs, tomatoes (coarsely chopped) and their liquid, and broth. Bring to a boil, cover, reduce heat, and boil gently until beans are nearly tender (30 to 40 minutes).

4. Stir in wine and pasta and boil gently, uncovered, until pasta is tender (10 to 12 minutes). Add spinach, stirring just until it is wilted. Taste, and add salt if needed.

5. Serve with Parmesan cheese to sprinkle over each serving to taste.

Makes 12 to 14 cups, 4 to 6 servings.

OLD-FASHIONED NAVY BEAN SOUP

Good accompaniments for this traditional, thick soup are crisp coleslaw, corn muffins, and a luscious homemade dessert such as an apple pie.

 1 pound (about 2½ cups)
   dried small white beans,
   rinsed and drained
 8 cups water
 4 smoked ham hocks (2½ to
   3 lbs)
 1 large onion, finely chopped
 1 bay leaf
 3 whole cloves
 ½ teaspoon sugar
 2 stalks celery, with leaves,
   finely chopped
 1 carrot, shredded
 ⅛ teaspoon white pepper
   Salt (optional)

1. Place beans in a large bowl; add 2 teaspoons salt and 6 cups water. Cover and let stand for at least 8 hours. Drain and discard soaking liquid. Or, to shorten the soaking period, place beans in a 3- to 4-quart pan with 8 cups water (*no salt*); bring to a boil; then boil briskly, uncovered, for 2 minutes. Remove from heat, cover, and let stand for 1 hour. Drain, discarding liquid.

2. In a 5- to 6-quart kettle, combine drained beans, the 8 cups water, ham hocks, onion, bay leaf, cloves, sugar, celery, carrot, and pepper. Bring to a boil over medium heat. Cover, reduce heat, and boil gently until beans are very tender and soup begins to thicken (4 to 5 hours).

3. Remove and discard bay leaf. Remove ham hocks. When they are cool enough to handle, discard bones and skin; return ham in large chunks to soup. Taste, and add salt if needed.

4. Reheat if necessary; serve hot.

Makes about 10 cups, 6 servings.

SPLIT PEA SOUP, BLACK FOREST STYLE

Add fresh parsley and sliced green onions just before you serve this tangy pea soup dotted with veal frankfurter slices. Accompany it with light rye bread, red and green cabbage slaw with sour cream dressing, and tart red apples for dessert. Beer or, better yet, an Alsatian Gewürztraminer is a good beverage to go with the soup.

2 tablespoons butter or margarine
2 medium onions, finely chopped
2 medium carrots, diced
1 stalk celery, thinly sliced
1 medium potato (about ½ lb), diced
1 large smoked ham hock (about 1 lb) or a meaty ham bone
1 package (12 oz; about 1⅓ cups) green split peas, rinsed and drained
1 can or bottle (12 oz) beer
6 cups water
1 teaspoon dried thyme
2 teaspoons whole mustard seed, crushed
⅛ teaspoon ground cloves
½ pound veal frankfurters, sliced ½ inch thick
2 tablespoons cider vinegar
Salt (optional)
¼ cup each chopped parsley and sliced green onions

1. In a 5½- to 6-quart kettle over medium heat, melt butter. Add onions, carrots, and celery and cook, stirring occasionally, until vegetables are soft but not browned.

2. Add potato, ham hock, split peas, beer, the water, thyme, mustard seed, and cloves. Bring to a boil, cover, reduce heat, and simmer, stirring occasionally, until ham and peas are very tender (2 to 2½ hours).

3. Remove ham hock. When it is cool enough to handle, remove and discard bones and skin. Return meat to soup in large chunks.

4. Add frankfurter slices and reheat to serving temperature. Blend in vinegar. Taste, and add salt if needed. Stir in parsley and green onions, and serve at once.

Makes about 12 cups, 6 servings.

The flavors of split peas, veal frankfurters, and vegetables meld together to produce a robust Split Pea Soup, Black Forest Style.

TURKEY AND CHICKEN SOUPS

The economical chicken is the versatile star of many kinds of dishes—not the least of which is soup. Without making claims as to the medicinal value of chicken soup, one can say that such good fare as the chicken soups that follow is certainly a tonic for lagging appetites or spirits.

Turkey, too, can be counted among the truly good buys for your grocery dollar.

TURKEY GARBURE

Garbure, a soup of long-standing tradition in the Southwest of France, is usually made with duck or goose. In these weight-conscious times, turkey is a lighter choice—and it is more easily come by, too. Turkey teams well with such time-honored ingredients as dried white beans, turnips, and cabbage. Serve this lusty soup with a rough, country-style bread, sliced or cherry tomatoes, and a red jug wine.

    1   cup small white beans,
        rinsed and drained
    3   leeks
    2   tablespoons butter or
        margarine
    2   medium onions, chopped
    3   cloves garlic, minced
        or pressed
    1   teaspoon each dried thyme
        and marjoram
    ¼   teaspoon white pepper
    1   large smoked ham hock (1 to
        1½ lbs) or a meaty ham bone
 2½ to 3 pounds turkey drumsticks
        or thighs
    3   medium potatoes (1 to
        1¼ lbs), diced
    3   medium carrots, sliced
    3   small turnips, cut in quarters,
        then sliced
    ½   cup chopped parsley
    1   bay leaf
   10   cups water
    1   small cabbage (about 1 lb),
        cut in thin wedges
    3   tablespoons red wine vinegar
        Salt (optional)

1. Place beans in a large bowl; add 1 teaspoon salt and 3 cups water. Cover and let stand for at least 8 hours; drain, discarding soaking liquid. Or, to shorten the soaking period, place beans in a 2- to 3-quart pan with 4 cups water (*no salt*); bring to a boil; then boil briskly, uncovered, for 2 minutes. Remove from heat, cover, and let stand for 1 hour. Drain, discarding soaking liquid.

2. Cut off root ends of leeks; remove and discard coarse outer leaves. Cut off and discard green tops so that leeks are about 9 inches long. Split lengthwise, from leafy end, cutting to within about 1 inch of root end. Soak in cold water for several minutes; then separate leaves under running water to rinse away any clinging grit; drain. Slice about ¼ inch thick.

3. In a 7½- to 8-quart kettle over medium heat, melt butter. Add leeks and onions and cook, stirring often, until soft but not browned. Stir in garlic, thyme, marjoram, and pepper. Then add drained beans, ham hock, turkey, potatoes, carrots, turnips, parsley, bay leaf, and the 10 cups water. Bring slowly to a boil; cover, and simmer until beans and turkey are very tender (3½ to 4 hours).

4. Remove and discard bay leaf. Remove turkey and ham hock from soup. Scoop out about 3 cups beans and vegetables with a little broth; purée in blender or food processor until smooth. When turkey and ham are cool enough to handle, remove meat in chunks and return it to soup; discard bones, skin, and fat. Skim and discard surface fat from soup.

5. Stir bean purée into soup and cook over medium heat until soup boils gently. Add cabbage and cook, uncovered, stirring occasionally, until cabbage is tender and bright green (8 to 10 minutes).

6. Blend in vinegar; then taste, and add salt if needed. Serve hot.

Makes about 6 quarts, 10 to 12 servings.

CURRIED TURKEY SOUP

Hard-cooked eggs, toasted coconut, and green onions accent this quick-cooking ground-turkey soup.

    3   tablespoons butter or
        margarine
 1½   pounds ground turkey,
        crumbled
    1   large onion, finely chopped
    4   teaspoons curry powder
    ½   teaspoon mustard seed,
        crushed
    1   medium carrot, shredded
    1   tart green apple, peeled, cored,
        and shredded
    2   cloves garlic, minced or
        pressed
    6   cups Rich Chicken Broth (see
        page 8) or 3 cans (14½ oz
        each) chicken broth
    1   cup whipping cream
    ½   cup shelled fresh or
        frozen peas
    2   egg yolks
    1   teaspoon grated lemon rind
        Salt (optional)
        Sieved hard-cooked egg,
        toasted shredded coconut,
        and thinly sliced green
        onions, for garnish

1. In a 3½- to 4-quart saucepan over medium heat, melt butter. Add turkey and cook, stirring often, until it loses its pink color. Add onion, curry powder, and mustard seed; cook, stirring often, until onion is soft. Mix in carrot, apple, and garlic.

2. Add broth. Bring slowly to a boil, cover, reduce heat, and simmer for 40 minutes.

3. Add cream and peas and cook, uncovered, over medium heat until mixture is steaming and heated through (about 5 minutes). In a small bowl beat egg yolks. Blend in a little of the hot soup; then blend egg yolk mixture into soup. Stir constantly over low heat until soup begins to thicken. *Do not boil.* Stir in lemon rind; taste, and add salt if needed.

4. Serve with small bowls of sieved egg, coconut, and green onions to garnish each serving to taste.

Makes about 12 cups, 6 servings.

MAJORCAN CHICKEN AND SAUSAGE SOUP

Serve this Spanish soup with a salad of greens, oranges, and red onions, and a light red wine or Mexican beer.

    2 tablespoons olive oil
    1 medium carrot, shredded
    1 large onion, thinly slivered
    1 stalk celery, thinly sliced
    1 clove garlic, minced or pressed
    1 chicken (3 to 3½ lbs), cut up
       (including giblets)
       Pinch saffron threads or
       powder
    1 teaspoon salt
    1 can (1 lb) tomatoes
    6 cups water
    ½ pound chorizo sausages
    ¼ cup tiny star-shaped pasta
    ¼ cup coarsely chopped cilantro
       (Chinese parsley)

1. In a 4- to 5-quart kettle, heat olive oil over moderate heat. Add carrot, onion, and celery and cook, stirring often, until onion is soft but not browned. Stir in garlic.

2. Add chicken pieces (including neck, heart, and gizzard; reserve liver to cook later) and sprinkle with saffron and salt. Add tomatoes (coarsely chopped) with their liquid and the water. Bring to a boil, cover, reduce heat, and simmer until chicken is very tender and broth is flavorful (2 to 2½ hours).

3. Remove chicken pieces; discard bones and skin, and separate meat into large chunks. Chop heart and gizzard finely. (This can all be done ahead of time; wrap and refrigerate the meat and soup separately.)

4. Shortly before serving, remove casings and slice chorizos about ¼ inch thick. In a medium frying pan, brown lightly in their own drippings. Remove from pan and drain on paper towels, reserving drippings.

5. Skim off and discard fat from surface of broth. Bring soup slowly to a boil over medium heat. Add pasta and the browned sausage and cook, uncovered, until pasta is nearly tender (10 to 12 minutes). Meanwhile, cut chicken liver in half and brown quickly in reserved sausage drippings. Cut liver pieces into ¼-inch-wide strips.

6. Return chicken to soup and cook until heated through (about 5 minutes). Mix in liver strips. Taste, and add salt if needed.

7. Stir in cilantro and serve at once.

Makes 10 to 12 cups, 4 to 6 servings.

CHICKEN SOUP PROVENÇALE

Fresh fennel flavors this handsome chicken soup. Use the lower, bulb-shaped portion of each feathery-fronded stalk. If fennel is not available, increase the celery to two stalks and add ⅛ teaspoon fennel or anise seed (finely crushed). Serve the soup with French bread, crisp radishes on a bed of ice, and a light red wine.

    1 leek
    2 tablespoons olive oil
    2 medium carrots, chopped
    1 medium onion, finely chopped
    1 stalk celery, thinly sliced
    ½ cup chopped fresh fennel
    1 clove garlic, minced or pressed
    1 chicken (3 to 3½ lbs), cut up
       (reserve giblets for other uses)
    ½ cup chopped fresh basil leaves
       or 2 tablespoons dried basil
    1 teaspoon salt
    ⅛ teaspoon white pepper
    7 cups water
    ¼ teaspoon saffron threads or
       powder
    3 medium tomatoes, peeled,
       seeded, and chopped
    1 tablespoon anise-flavored
       apéritif (such as Pernod or
       Ricard), optional

1. Cut off root end of leek; remove and discard coarse outer leaves. Cut off and discard green top so that leek is about 9 inches long. Split lengthwise from leafy end, cutting to within about 1 inch of root end. Soak in cold water for several minutes; then separate leaves under running water to rinse away any clinging grit; drain. Slice about ¼ inch thick.

2. In a 4- to 5-quart kettle heat olive oil over moderate heat. Add leek, carrots, onion, celery, and fennel and cook, stirring often, until onion is soft but not browned. Stir in garlic. Add chicken pieces; then sprinkle with half of the basil and the salt and pepper. Add the water. Bring to a boil, cover, reduce heat, and simmer until chicken is very tender and broth is flavorful (2 to 2½ hours).

3. Remove chicken pieces; discard bones and skin, and separate meat into large chunks. (All this can be done well ahead of time; wrap and refrigerate chicken, and cover and refrigerate soup.)

4. Skim off and discard fat from surface of broth. Bring soup slowly to a boil over medium heat. Remove about ⅓ cup of the broth and stir saffron into it; let stand for 5 minutes. Add tomatoes and remaining basil to soup; then add saffron mixture. Return chicken to soup and cook until heated through (about 5 minutes). Taste; add salt if needed.

5. Blend in apéritif (if used) and serve at once.

Makes 11 to 12 cups, 6 servings.

Chicken and Tortellini Soup is easy to prepare and makes a satisfying meal. Check out the frozen foods section in your supermarket—frozen tortellini are often available. Many markets also sell dried tortellini.

CHICKEN AND TORTELLINI SOUP

This quick soup combines chicken with tortellini, the fetchingly shaped stuffed pasta. (One Italian legend has it that they were modeled after the navel of Venus.) If you can't get tortellini, you might substitute plain, unsauced ravioli.

- 4 each *chicken legs and thighs* (2¼ to 2½ lbs)
- 2 tablespoons *olive oil*
- 2 medium *onions, slivered*
- 1 stalk *celery, thinly sliced*
- 2 medium *carrots, chopped*
- 1 large *clove garlic, minced or pressed*
- 1 teaspoon *dried basil*
- ½ teaspoon *dried oregano*
- ¼ teaspoon each *dried thyme and sage*
- 1 large *can (28 oz) tomatoes*
- 1¾ cups *Rich Chicken Broth (see page 8)* or *1 can (14½ oz) chicken broth*
- 1 cup *dry red wine*
- 1 can (8 oz) *tomato sauce*
- 1 package (12 oz) *frozen tortellini*
- 3 cups *slivered chard or spinach leaves (discard coarse stems)*
  Salt (optional)
  Grated Parmesan cheese

1. In a 4½- to 5-quart Dutch oven, heat olive oil over medium heat. Add chicken pieces, about half at a time, and brown on all sides, removing them as they brown. Pour off all but about 2 tablespoons of the drippings. To same pan add onions, celery, and carrots. Cook, stirring often, until soft but not browned. Stir in garlic. Return chicken to pan.

2. Sprinkle with basil, oregano, thyme, and sage. Mix in tomatoes (coarsely chopped) with their liquid, broth, wine, and tomato sauce. Bring to a boil, cover, reduce heat, and simmer until chicken is tender and broth is flavorful (about 1 hour).

3. Meanwhile, cook tortellini in boiling salted water according to package directions. Rinse with cold water, drain well, and reserve.

4. Mix cooked tortellini and slivered chard into soup and cook, uncovered, until chard is wilted and bright green and tortellini are heated (3 to 5 minutes). Taste; add salt if needed.

5. Serve in broad, shallow bowls with Parmesan cheese to sprinkle over each serving to taste.

Makes about 15 cups, 4 to 6 servings.

MINTED CHICKEN AND GARBANZO SOUP

The hot flavor of red chile contrasts with the cool freshness of mint.

> 1 cup dried garbanzos, rinsed and drained
> 1 teaspoon salt
> 2 tablespoons olive oil
> 1 large onion, finely chopped
> 1 stalk celery, thinly sliced
> 2 cloves garlic, minced
> 1 bay leaf
> 1 small dried hot red chile, crushed
> ½ cup chopped fresh mint leaves or 2 tablespoons dried mint
> 6 cups water
> 1 chicken (3 to 3½ lbs), cut up (save giblets for other uses)
> 1 large can (28 oz) tomatoes
> Salt (optional)

1. Place beans in a bowl; add the 1 teaspoon salt and 3 cups water. Cover and let stand for at least 8 hours; drain, discarding soaking liquid.

2. In a 5½- to 6-quart kettle, heat oil. Add onion and celery and cook, stirring often, until soft but not browned. Mix in garlic, bay leaf, chile, and half of the mint; add drained beans and the 6 cups water. Bring to a boil, cover, reduce heat; boil gently for 1 hour.

3. Add chicken pieces and tomatoes (coarsely chopped) and their liquid. Return to a gentle boil, cover, reduce heat, and simmer until chicken and beans are tender (about 2 hours).

4. Remove chicken pieces and let cool slightly; remove meat in chunks, discarding bones and skin. Set aside.

5. Scoop out about 2 cups of the cooked beans and tomatoes with a little of the cooking liquid. Place in blender or food processor and whirl or process until smoothly puréed. Mix into soup; then add chicken. Taste, and add salt if needed.

6. Reheat soup to serving temperature. Blend in remaining mint, stir for about 1 minute, and serve hot.

Makes 12 to 14 cups, 6 servings.

CHICKEN AND POTATO SOUP PICCANTE

Lavish Cheddar cheese over this chicken soup, and serve it with sesame-sprinkled homemade muffins, crisp raw vegetables, and beer.

> 2 tablespoons butter
> 1 medium onion, finely chopped
> 1 red bell pepper, seeded and chopped
> 1 stalk celery, thinly sliced
> 1 clove garlic, minced or pressed
> 1 can (4 oz) diced green chiles
> 4 medium-sized, smooth-skinned potatoes (1½ to 2 lbs), diced
> 1 chicken (3 to 3½ lbs), cut up (save giblets for other uses)
> ½ teaspoon dried thyme
> 1 teaspoon salt
> 7 cups water
> Grated Cheddar cheese, for garnish

1. In a 5- to 6-quart kettle over medium heat, melt butter. Add onion, bell pepper, and celery and cook, stirring occasionally, until onion is soft but not browned.

2. Mix in garlic, green chiles, and potatoes. Add chicken pieces. Sprinkle with thyme and salt. Add the water. Bring slowly to a boil, cover, reduce heat, and simmer until chicken is very tender and broth is flavorful (2 to 2½ hours).

3. Remove chicken pieces; when cool, discard bones and skin, and separate meat into chunks.

4. Scoop out about 2 cups of vegetables from soup with a little of the broth; purée in blender or food processor until smooth. Return purée to soup. Skim and discard surface fat. Add chicken and cook, occasionally stirring gently, until heated through. Taste, and add salt if needed.

5. Serve hot soup with cheese to sprinkle over each serving to taste.

Makes about 12 cups, 6 servings.

CHICKEN AND MEATBALL SOUP

Accompany this satisfying chicken soup with a salad of young greens.

> 1 chicken (3 to 3½ lbs), cut up (save giblets for other uses)
> 1 stalk celery, thinly sliced
> 1 large carrot, chopped
> 1 large onion, finely chopped
> 1 teaspoon salt
> 1 bay leaf
> ½ teaspoon dried thyme
> ¼ teaspoon dried sage
> 7 cups water
> Grated Parmesan cheese

Veal and Pork Meatballs

> 1 egg
> ¼ cup each soft bread crumbs and grated Parmesan cheese
> ¾ teaspoon salt
> ¼ teaspoon dried marjoram
> Pinch ground nutmeg
> 1 small clove garlic, minced
> ¼ cup finely chopped parsley
> ½ pound each ground veal and ground pork

1. In a 5- to 6-quart kettle, combine chicken, celery, carrot, onion, salt, bay leaf, thyme, sage, and the water. Bring slowly to a boil; cover, reduce heat, and simmer until chicken is very tender (2 to 2½ hours).

2. Remove chicken. Cool, bone, skin, and separate meat into large chunks.

3. Prepare Veal and Pork Meatballs.

4. Skim and discard fat. Bring soup to a boil over medium heat. Add meatballs, a few at a time. Cook, uncovered, until they rise to the surface. Cover; simmer 5 minutes. Add chicken and cook just until heated through. Taste; add salt if needed.

5. Serve in broad, shallow bowls with Parmesan cheese.

Makes about 12 cups, 6 servings.

Veal and Pork Meatballs In a medium bowl beat egg; mix in bread crumbs, Parmesan cheese, salt, marjoram, nutmeg, and garlic. Lightly mix in parsley, veal, and pork. Shape into 1-inch meatballs.

WINTER AVOCADO FEAST

Guacamole With Crisp
Raw Vegetables and
Corn Chips

Mexican Chicken and
Avocado Soup

Warm Corn Bread

Butter

Berry Sherbet

Pecan Polvorones

Beer

Coffee

When avocados are in season, schedule this menu that showcases the fruit in two courses. Start with your favorite guacamole, then continue with soup in the style of the seaside resort of Ixtapa.

The cookies are typical of the treats sold in Oaxacan bakeries.

MEXICAN CHICKEN AND AVOCADO SOUP

1 chicken (3 to 3½ lbs), cut up
  (reserve giblets for other uses)
1 stalk celery, thinly sliced
2 medium carrots, chopped
2 medium onions, slivered
1 large clove garlic, minced
  or pressed
1 teaspoon each *salt* and *whole
  cumin seed, crushed*
½ teaspoon dried oregano
2 small dried red chiles, crushed
6 cups water
2 cups cut green beans (fresh
  or frozen)
2 medium tomatoes, seeded
  and chopped
¼ cup chopped fresh cilantro
  (Chinese parsley)
1 large avocado, peeled, seeded,
  and thinly sliced
  Lime wedges, for garnish

1. In a 5- to 6-quart kettle or Dutch oven, combine chicken, celery, carrots, onions, garlic, salt, cumin seed, oregano, chiles, and the water. Bring slowly to a boil; then cover, reduce heat, and simmer until chicken is very tender and broth is flavorful (2 to 2½ hours).

2. Remove chicken pieces; discard bones and skin, and separate meat into chunks. (This can all be done ahead of time; wrap and refrigerate meat; cover and refrigerate soup.)

3. Skim and discard fat from broth. Bring soup to a boil, add green beans, and cook, uncovered, for 5 minutes. Add chicken, reduce heat, and cook until it is heated through (3 to 5 minutes). Taste, and add salt if needed. Gently stir in tomatoes, cilantro, and avocado slices.

4. Serve with lime wedges to squeeze into each portion of soup to taste.

Makes about 12 cups, 6 servings.

PECAN POLVORONES

½ cup butter or margarine,
  softened
½ cup lard, at room
  temperature
¾ cup sugar
1 egg yolk
1 teaspoon vanilla extract
2¼ cups flour
½ teaspoon ground
  cinnamon
  Pinch salt
½ cup finely chopped pecans
  Additional sugar

1. Preheat oven to 350° F. In a large bowl cream softened butter and lard with the ¾ cup sugar. Beat until fluffy. Beat in egg yolk and vanilla until well combined.

2. In another bowl stir together flour, cinnamon, and salt until they are well blended. Gradually add the flour mixture to the creamed mixture, beating until well combined. Blend in chopped pecans.

3. To form each cookie, shape dough into a ball the size of a small walnut. Roll the ball in sugar until it is generously coated all over. Place cookies on ungreased baking sheets. Using a glass dipped in sugar, flatten each cookie into rounds that are approximately ½ inch thick.

4. Bake for 10 minutes; then reduce heat to 300° F and continue baking until cookies are lightly browned (12 to 15 minutes). Leave cookies on the baking sheet until they have cooled slightly (hot cookies break easily); then transfer them to wire racks to cool completely.

Makes about 3 dozen cookies.

Cooking avocados ruins the texture, and too much heat tends to make them taste bitter. Therefore, add sliced avocado just before you serve the soup.

THREE WAYS TO MAKE CHINESE CHICKEN SOUP

A fragrantly steaming bowl of soup is a favorite opener for a Chinese meal. On tasting these subtle flavors and brilliantly colored tidbits, many Westerners wish they could make an entire meal of such a soup.

Although it may not be traditional, there is no reason not to do just that. Here is a recipe for a basic chicken soup that can be turned into your choice of colorful Chicken Corn Soup, peppery Hot-and-Sour Soup, or dramatic Sizzling Rice Soup. This is a more substantial soup than you will find in a Chinese restaurant (where just the meaty bones of chicken used in other dishes flavor the broth).

Sizzling Rice Soup gets its name from the addition of the dry crust that forms on the bottom of the rice pot. However, you can also cook rice and then dry it in the oven before frying.

CHINESE CHICKEN STOCK

- 1 chicken (3 to 3½ lbs), cut up (discard giblets)
- 2 slices (about ¼ in. thick) peeled fresh ginger, slivered
- 3 green onions, chopped
- 1 clove garlic, sliced
- 1 teaspoon salt
- 6 cups water
- 1 small dried red chile, coarsely crushed, for Hot-and-Sour Soup only (see Note)

1. In a 5- to 6-quart kettle, combine chicken, ginger, green onions, garlic, salt, and the water. If you will be making Hot-and-Sour Soup, add the crushed chile. Bring slowly to a boil; then cover, reduce heat, and simmer until chicken is very tender and broth is flavorful (2 to 2½ hours).

2. Remove chicken pieces; when cool, discard bones and skin, and dice or shred meat (reserve meat for soup). Strain broth, discarding seasonings. (This can all be done ahead of time; wrap and refrigerate meat, and cover and refrigerate soup.)

CHICKEN CORN SOUP

- Chinese Chicken Stock
- ¼ teaspoon Oriental chili oil (see Note)
- 1 medium carrot, quartered lengthwise, then thinly sliced
- 1½ to 2 cups fresh corn kernels (cut from 2 medium ears)
- ½ cup shelled fresh or frozen peas
- Cooked chicken meat (reserved from stock)
- 1 tablespoon cornstarch
- 2 tablespoons water
- 2 eggs
- Salt to taste
- 3 tablespoons thinly sliced green onion, for garnish

1. Skim and discard fat from surface of Chinese Chicken Stock. Reheat stock in kettle over medium heat. Add chili oil and carrot. Cover and boil gently for 5 minutes.

2. Stir in corn and peas; cook, uncovered, for 3 minutes.

3. Mix in cooked chicken. In a small bowl blend cornstarch smoothly with the water. Blend into soup, stirring until soup boils and becomes clear.

4. In a medium bowl beat eggs. Remove soup pan from heat. Add eggs to soup slowly, stirring constantly, until they form long threads. Taste, and add salt if needed. To serve, sprinkle soup with green onions.

Makes 10 to 12 cups, 6 servings.

HOT-AND-SOUR SOUP

- Chinese Chicken Stock
- 4 large dried Chinese mushrooms (see Note)
- 1 loin pork chop, ¾ inch thick (about ½ lb)
- ½ cup matchstick-sliced canned bamboo shoots
- Cooked chicken meat (reserved from stock)
- ½ cup diced tofu (see Note)
- ¼ pound peeled tiny shrimp
- ¼ cup rice wine vinegar (see Note)
- 1 tablespoon each cornstarch, soy sauce, and water
- ½ teaspoon Chinese chili oil (see Note)
- ¼ teaspoon each white pepper and Oriental sesame oil (see Note)
- 2 eggs
- ⅓ cup thinly sliced green onions, for garnish

1. Skim and discard fat from surface of Chinese Chicken Stock; reheat stock in kettle over medium heat. Soak dried mushrooms in warm water to cover for 30 minutes; drain and squeeze dry. Cut off and discard stems. Cut caps into thin slivers. Trim meat from pork chop; cut meat in long, thin strips.

2. Add mushrooms, pork, and bamboo shoots to stock in kettle. Cover and simmer for 10 minutes. Add cooked chicken, tofu, and shrimp. Cook, uncovered, for 3 minutes.

3. Stir in vinegar. In a small bowl blend cornstarch with the soy sauce, water, chili oil, white pepper, and Oriental sesame oil. Blend cornstarch mixture into soup, stirring until soup boils and becomes clear.

4. In a medium bowl beat eggs slightly. Remove pan from heat. Add eggs slowly to soup, stirring constantly, until they form long threads. Taste, and add salt if needed. To serve, sprinkle soup with green onion.

Makes 10 to 12 cups, 6 servings.

SIZZLING RICE SOUP

1½ cups water
⅔ cup short-grain rice
   Chinese Chicken Stock
1 stalk celery, thinly sliced
   on the diagonal
1 small onion, thinly sliced
¼ cup sliced water chestnuts
1 cup sliced fresh mushrooms
   Oil, for frying
1 cup snow peas
   Cooked chicken meat (reserved
   from stock)
1 tablespoon each soy sauce
   and dry sherry
1 teaspoon Oriental sesame
   oil (see Note)
   Salt to taste

1. In a small pan bring the water to a boil; add rice, cover, reduce heat, and simmer for 20 minutes. Remove pan from heat and let stand, covered, for 30 minutes. Then pat rice out evenly about ½ inch thick on a greased baking sheet. Dry in a 300° F oven until rice feels dry on surface (1 to 1½ hours). Break into bite-sized pieces. Set aside.

2. Skim and discard fat from surface of Chinese Chicken Stock. Reheat in kettle. Add celery, onion, water chestnuts, and mushrooms. Cover and boil gently for 5 minutes.

3. Meanwhile, pour salad oil into a deep, heavy frying pan or wok to a depth of 1 inch; heat to 375° F on a frying thermometer. Fry pieces of dried cooked rice, about half at a time, until golden brown (30 seconds to 1 minute). Drain; keep warm on an ovenproof plate in a 300° F oven.

4. Snap off ends and remove strings from snow peas. Add to soup with cooked chicken; cook, uncovered, until chicken is heated (3 to 5 minutes). Blend in soy sauce, sherry, and sesame oil. Salt to taste. Ladle into a warm bowl.

5. Ladle soup into bowls; then add 2 or 3 pieces of hot fried rice to each.

Makes 10 to 12 cups, 6 servings.

Note You can find these items in Oriental markets.

Soup is not generally served as a main dish in China. However, since these recipes are so complete in all the elements that Westerners expect, why not enjoy them as a meal?

SOUPS WITH FISH

There are some who might argue that the Breton Mussel and Shrimp Soup With Rice in this section is a stew—and they would not be incorrect. The line separating a soup from a stew becomes very thin where fish is involved. The "soups" that follow include generous amounts to chew as well as broth to drink.

It used to be a bit of a joke to refer to men's formal wear as a soup-and-fish. When dinners followed a rigid pattern of set courses, the dress code was just as stiffly predictable. None of the soups ahead can be described by such adjectives as formal, rigid, stiff, or predictable.

These fish soups all entice with surprising, light-hearted flavors. The two creamy chowders don't require much time to prepare, yet each can be served as the centerpiece of a special dinner.

CREAMY SALMON CHOWDER

The flavors of a sumptuous baked salmon dish at Chef Alain Dutournier's Paris restaurant, Au Trou Gascon, inspired this suave salmon chowder. Serve it as a main course with a salad of mushrooms and young greens, followed by a nut ice cream and crisp cookies for dessert.

- 3 tablespoons butter or margarine
- 4 shallots, slivered (about ¾ cup)
- 1 teaspoon dried tarragon
- 3 medium-sized, smooth-skinned potatoes (about 1½ lbs), thinly sliced
- ½ teaspoon salt
- ⅛ teaspoon white pepper
- 2 cups Fish Broth (see page 11) or Rich Chicken Broth (see page 8) or 1 can (14½ oz) chicken broth
- 1½ pounds salmon steaks, ¾ to 1 inch thick

- 1 lemon, thinly sliced
- 1 bay leaf
- 1 cup dry white wine
- ¼ pound sliced bacon, cut in ½-inch-wide pieces
- Half a small cabbage, cored and thinly shredded (about 4 cups)
- 1 cup whipping cream

1. In a heavy 4- to 5-quart saucepan or Dutch oven over medium heat, melt butter. Add shallots and cook, stirring, until soft but not browned. Mix in tarragon.

2. Add potatoes. Sprinkle with salt and pepper. Add broth and bring to a boil. Cover, reduce heat, and boil gently for 15 minutes.

3. Add salmon steaks in a single layer; cover with lemon slices; then add bay leaf. Pour in wine. Cover again and cook over low heat until salmon flakes when tested with a fork and potatoes are tender (10 to 12 minutes). Meanwhile, in a medium frying pan, cook bacon in its own drippings until lightly browned. Remove from heat, drain on paper towel, and keep warm.

4. Remove and discard bay leaf and lemon slices. Remove salmon steaks; discard salmon bones and skin and divide salmon into chunks. Add cabbage and cream to soup. Stir occasionally over medium heat until cabbage is wilted and bright green (3 to 5 minutes). Gently mix in salmon. Taste, and add salt if needed.

5. Serve chowder hot, spooning several pieces of bacon into each bowl.

Makes 10 to 12 cups, 4 to 6 servings.

RED-AND-WHITE FISH CHOWDER

This colorful chowder is not difficult to prepare and comes together quickly. The Crisp Bread Sticks on page 74 are a good accompaniment.

- ¼ cup butter or margarine
- 1 large onion, thinly slivered
- 1 stalk celery, thinly sliced
- 1 red bell pepper, seeded and chopped
- ½ teaspoon dried thyme
- 3 medium-sized red-skinned potatoes (about 1½ lbs), scrubbed and diced (unpeeled)
- ½ teaspoon salt
- ⅛ teaspoon white pepper
- 2 cups Fish Broth (see page 11) or Rich Chicken Broth (see page 8) or 1 can (14½ oz) chicken broth
- 1½ pounds red snapper fillets, cut crosswise in 1-inch-wide strips
- ¼ pound sliced pancetta or bacon, cut in ½-inch-wide pieces
- 2 cups half-and-half

1. In a heavy 3½- to 4-quart saucepan over medium heat, melt butter. Add onion, celery, and bell pepper and cook, stirring, until onion is soft but not browned. Mix in thyme.

2. Add potatoes. Sprinkle with salt and pepper. Add broth and bring to a boil. Cover, reduce heat, and boil gently for 15 minutes.

3. Add fish strips, cover again, and cook over low heat until fish flakes when tested with a fork and potatoes are tender (8 to 10 minutes). Meanwhile, in a medium frying pan, cook pancetta in its own drippings until lightly browned. Remove from heat, drain, and keep warm.

4. Stir half-and-half gently into the soup and cook, stirring occasionally, just until steaming hot. *Do not boil.*

5. Serve hot, spooning several pieces of pancetta into each bowl.

Makes about 10 cups, 4 to 6 servings.

CHEESE-CRUSTED FISH SOUP

This thick, red fish soup with a broiled topping of toasted croutons and cheese synthesizes several *soupes de poissons* enjoyed on the Atlantic coast of France.

For the best results, make sure that the fish you use is fresh and tasty. See "Shopping for Fish" (at right) for tips on how to ensure that it is.

To turn this soup into a meal, add a green vegetable salad—asparagus, broccoli, or green beans in a vinaigrette dressing—and drink a light red wine with the soup.

    3 tablespoons olive oil
    1 medium onion, thinly slivered
    1 stalk celery, thinly sliced
    1 red bell pepper, seeded and
       chopped
    3 cloves garlic
    1 small dried hot red chile,
       crushed
    ½ teaspoon each salt, dried
       thyme, and dried basil
    ⅛ teaspoon anise or fennel
       seed, crushed
       Pinch ground cloves
    1 large can (28 oz) tomatoes
    ¼ cup tomato paste
    2 cups Fish Broth (see
       page 11) or Rich Chicken
       Broth (see page 8) or 1 can
       (14½ oz) chicken broth
    1 cup dry white wine
    6 slices French bread, about
       ½ inch thick
    6 tablespoons grated Parmesan
       cheese
    1 pound lingcod steaks
    1 to 1½ pounds sea bass fillets,
       cut in 1-inch-wide strips
    ½ pound peeled tiny cooked
       shrimp
    ¼ cup chopped parsley
    ½ pound Swiss cheese, shredded
       (about 2 cups)

1. In a 4- to 5-quart kettle or Dutch oven, heat olive oil over medium heat. Add onion, celery, and bell pepper and cook, stirring often, until onion is soft but not browned. Mince or press 2 of the garlic cloves and add to the onion mixture together with chile, salt, thyme, basil, anise seed, and cloves.

2. Mix in the tomatoes (coarsely chopped) and their liquid, tomato paste, broth, and wine. Bring to a boil, cover, reduce heat, and simmer for 45 minutes.

3. Meanwhile, place bread slices on a baking sheet. Peel remaining clove of garlic and cut it in half. Use the cut clove of garlic to rub both sides of each slice of bread. Bake sliced bread in a 325° F oven until crisp and lightly browned (40 to 45 minutes). Sprinkle each slice with 1 tablespoon of the Parmesan cheese.

4. Remove and discard skin and large central bone from each lingcod steak, cut fish in chunks, and add to soup. Simmer, uncovered, for 20 minutes. Then add sea bass fillets and shrimp. Cook over medium heat, uncovered, stirring occasionally, just until sea bass flakes when tested with a fork (3 to 5 minutes). Taste, and add salt if needed. Mix in parsley.

5. Preheat broiler. Divide soup among individual ovenproof bowls. Top each serving with a slice of toasted French bread. Divide Swiss cheese evenly over the bread. Place bowls on a baking sheet about 6 inches below broiler. Broil until cheese bubbles and browns lightly (6 to 8 minutes) and serve immediately.

Makes about 12 cups, 6 servings.

SHOPPING FOR FISH

Fresh fish and shellfish are critical to the success of a recipe. The most reliable way to make sure you are getting the best quality is to buy from a reputable fish dealer.

A fresh fish should not smell fishy. It should have a mild odor; firm, elastic flesh that springs back when it is pressed; clear, protruding eyes; reddish or pink gills; and scales that are shiny and bright as well as tight to the skin.

When buying steaks or fillets, look for flesh with a natural sheen; avoid pieces that are yellowish in color or ones that are brown around the edges. If the fish has been frozen, ask how long it has been defrosted. If the answer is longer than two days, do not buy it.

The flesh of shellfish should be firm and have a sweet smell. Any hint of ammonia is an indication of deterioration.

Oysters, clams, and mussels should be alive when purchased. The shells should be tightly closed or close when tapped on the counter.

CURRIED SCALLOP AND LEEK SOUP

This rich, golden soup is intended as a main dish, but in smaller portions it can also be served as a first course.

3 *leeks*
3 *tablespoons butter*
2 *shallots, finely chopped*
2 *teaspoons curry powder*
¼ *teaspoon ground ginger*
  Pinch cayenne pepper
2 *cloves garlic, minced*
1 *pound scallops (cut in half if large)*
3 *cups Fish Broth (see page 11) or Rich Chicken Broth (see page 8) or canned chicken broth*
1 *cup whipping cream*
2 *egg yolks*
2 *tablespoons lemon juice*
1 *cup dry white wine*
  Salt (optional)
  Sliced green onions, for garnish

1. Cut off root ends of leeks; remove and discard coarse outer leaves. Cut off and discard green tops. Split lengthwise, from leafy end, cutting to within about 1 inch of root end. Soak in cold water for several minutes; then separate leaves under running water to rinse away any clinging grit; drain. Slice about ¼ inch thick.

2. In a 3- to 4-quart pan over medium heat, melt butter. Cook leeks and shallots, stirring often, until leeks are soft but not browned. Stir in curry powder, ginger, cayenne, and garlic.

3. Add scallops, broth, and cream. Bring slowly to the boiling point; then cover, reduce heat, and simmer until scallops are opaque in center (about 5 minutes). Do not overcook them or scallops will be tough. Using a slotted spoon, remove scallops and reserve them.

4. In a small bowl beat egg yolks with lemon juice until blended.

5. Transfer soup mixture in which scallops cooked, about half at a time, to a blender or food processor, whirl or process until smooth, and return it to cooking pan. Blend wine into soup. Gradually add about ½ cup of the soup to egg yolk mixture, stir to blend, then add egg yolk mixture, all at once, to soup. Return scallops to soup. Stir over low heat until soup is steaming hot. *Do not boil.* Taste, and add salt if needed.

6. Serve soup hot, garnished with a sprinkling of green onion slices.

Makes about 8 cups, 4 servings.

BRETON MUSSEL AND SHRIMP SOUP WITH RICE

Cleaning, cooking, and shelling fresh mussels and shrimp for this crimson soup is a bit of a job, but the delicious results are well worth the work.

Finding a source of mussels used to be a problem. With the proliferation of fish markets and specialty supermarkets, this is no longer true.

This soup makes a very satisfying meal. Serve it with a whole-grain bread, sweet butter, and a dry white wine such as Muscadet.

1½ *cups water*
2½ *cups dry white wine*
1 *small onion, thinly sliced*
1 *stalk celery, coarsely chopped*
1 *bay leaf*
6 *sprigs parsley*
1 *teaspoon salt*
¼ *teaspoon black peppercorns*
1 *tablespoon lemon juice*
1 *pound fresh shrimp (in shells)*
2 *quarts (about 3 lbs) uncooked mussels in shells*
¼ *teaspoon white peppercorns*
1½ *to 2 cups Fish Broth (see page 11) or Rich Chicken Broth (see page 8) or 1 can (14½ oz) chicken broth*
⅛ *teaspoon saffron threads*
¼ *cup butter or margarine*
2 *shallots, finely chopped*
1 *medium onion, thinly slivered*
½ *pound mushrooms, thinly sliced*
1 *clove garlic, minced or pressed*
⅛ *teaspoon cayenne pepper*
1 *can (6 oz) tomato paste*
¼ *cup chopped parsley*
3 *cups hot cooked rice*

1. In a 3- to 4-quart saucepan or Dutch oven, combine the water with ½ cup of the wine, the small sliced onion, celery, bay leaf, 3 of the parsley sprigs, salt, black peppercorns, and lemon juice. Bring to a boil, cover, reduce heat, and simmer 5 minutes. Add shrimp. When mixture returns to a boil, remove pan from heat, cover, and let stand 10 minutes. Drain shrimp, reserving cooking liquid. (You should have about 2 cups shrimp and 2 cups liquid.) Peel and devein shrimp; set aside.

2. Discard any mussels that have opened and that do not close when rapped on the counter. Scrape off any barnacles; then scrub with a stiff brush under running water to remove sand; drain.

3. In a 4- to 5-quart kettle, combine mussels, remaining parsley sprigs, white peppercorns, and 1 cup of the wine. Bring to a boil over medium heat, cover, reduce heat, and simmer until mussels have opened (6 to 8 minutes). Discard any mussels that have remained closed. (They are likely to be shells full of sand.)

4. Remove mussels from liquid, reserving liquid. Reserve a few mussels in shells for garnish. Remove remaining mussels from shells. (You should have about 2 cups.) Pinch out and discard the "beard" from any mussel that has one. Add mussels to shrimp; set them aside.

5. Strain mussel and shrimp cooking liquids through a dampened cloth. Measure the combined liquid. Add Fish Broth to make 6 cups.

6. Place saffron in a small bowl and add ¼ cup of the hot shellfish liquid. Set aside to steep.

7. In a 3½- to 4-quart pan over medium heat, melt butter. Add shallots, the medium slivered onion, and mushrooms and cook, stirring often, until soft and lightly browned. Mix in garlic, cayenne, and tomato paste. Add the shellfish liquid, saffron mixture, and remaining 1 cup wine.

8. Bring slowly just to a boil, stirring occasionally, until soup is steaming hot. Mix in cooked mussels and shrimp. Taste, and add salt if needed. Mix in chopped parsley. Serve soup hot over rice in broad, shallow soup bowls. Garnish with mussels in shells.

Makes 10 to 12 cups, 6 servings.

Lovers of shellfish will delight in this Breton Mussel and Shrimp Soup With Rice. The addition of saffron is not essential but it adds such a distinctive taste and color that it is most definitely recommended.

WARM-WEATHER SOUP DINNER

Tricolor Artichoke Salad

Sole in Mint Broth

French Bread

Butter

*Creamy Lime Sherbet
With Raspberries*

White Wine

Coffee

Hot soup is certainly a welcome meal in cold weather, and it's also a good choice for a warm evening. Consider this menu for one of those hot Indian summer days.

A colorful salad starts you off, followed by small sole fillets poached in less than 5 minutes in a minty broth. Finish with a lime sherbet.

TRICOLOR ARTICHOKE SALAD

>　1　*package (8 oz) frozen
　　　 artichoke bottoms*
　1½　*cups thinly sliced or coarsely
　　　 chopped radishes*
　　1　*tablespoon snipped fresh
　　　 chives or finely chopped
　　　 green onions*
　　6　*cups torn romaine leaves*
　　½　*cup (about 3 oz) crumbled
　　　 goat cheese (chèvre)*

Creamy Mustard Dressing

>　1　*egg yolk*
　1½　*tablespoons tarragon
　　　 wine vinegar*
　1½　*teaspoons Dijon mustard
　　　 Pinch each salt and cayenne
　　　 pepper*
　　1　*clove garlic, minced or pressed*
　⅓　*cup olive oil*

1. Cook artichoke bottoms according to package directions just until tender. Drain, rinse with cold water to stop cooking, and drain again.

2. Prepare Creamy Mustard Dressing.

3. Just before serving, in a small bowl mix radishes, half of the dressing, and chives. In another bowl lightly mix romaine, remaining dressing, and goat cheese.

4. To serve, divide the romaine mixture among 4 salad plates. Arrange a fourth of the artichoke bottoms on each plate. Fill artichoke bottoms with radish mixture, dividing it evenly. Serve at once.

Serves 4.

Creamy Mustard Dressing In a medium bowl mix egg yolk, vinegar, mustard, salt, cayenne, and garlic. Using a whisk or fork, slowly and gradually beat in oil until dressing is thick and creamy.

Makes about ½ cup.

SOLE IN MINT BROTH

>　2　*tablespoons butter or
　　　 margarine*
　　1　*medium onion, thinly slivered*
　　1　*medium carrot, thinly sliced*
　　1　*lemon*
　　1　*small clove garlic, minced
　　　 or pressed*
　¼　*teaspoon white peppercorns*
　　1　*small bay leaf*
　½　*teaspoon salt*
　　1　*cup dry white wine*
　　3　*cups Fish Broth (see
　　　 page 11) or Rich Chicken
　　　 Broth (see page 8) or canned
　　　 chicken broth*
　　1　*pound small sole fillets*
　¾　*cup coarsely chopped fresh
　　　 mint leaves*

1. In a large, deep frying pan over medium heat, melt butter. Add onion and carrot and cook, stirring often, until soft but not browned.

2. Using a lemon stripper or small knife, remove rind from lemon in vertical strips. (Reserve strips to use in drinks if you wish.) Then cut lemon in half lengthwise and slice each half thinly.

3. Add lemon slices to onion mixture with garlic, peppercorns, bay leaf, salt, wine, and broth. Bring to a boil, cover, reduce heat, and simmer for 20 minutes.

4. Add fish fillets to liquid, cover, and cook gently over medium heat (liquid should barely bubble) for 2 minutes. Sprinkle with mint and continue cooking, uncovered, gently spooning broth over fish, just until fish is opaque and begins to separate into flakes when tested with a fork (2 to 3 minutes). Taste; add salt if needed.

5. Use a slotted spoon to transfer fish fillets to warm, broad, shallow soup bowls. Ladle broth over them.

Serves 4.

CREAMY LIME SHERBET

4 large limes (about ¾ lb)
  Lemon juice, if needed
2 cups half-and-half
1 cup sugar
  Few drops green food
  coloring (optional)
  Raspberries, for garnish

1. Grate about 3 tablespoons lime rind. Set aside. Squeeze limes and measure the juice. Add lemon juice, if needed, to make ½ cup.

2. In a medium bowl stir half-and-half with sugar until sugar dissolves. Mix in lime rind and juice. Blend in food coloring to tint mixture a pale green if you wish. Freeze in a loaf pan until firm (3 to 4 hours).

3. Remove sherbet from freezer and break up with a spoon; then transfer to a bowl and beat with an electric mixer until fluffy. Place in a covered container, return to freezer, and freeze again until firm (several hours or overnight).

4. Scoop into chilled dishes to serve. Add a handful of raspberries to decorate each serving.

Makes about 3 cups.

If raspberries are in season, use them to top a homemade lime sherbet. They will complement the elegant flavors and textures of poached sole and tender artichokes.

HOME-BAKED SOUP ACCOMPANIMENTS

Soup and crackers is one of those pairings of foods that seem so right it's hard to think of one without the other. The two are natural opposites, the crispness of the cracker contrasting with the smoothness of the soup. Packaged crackers are to be found in ever-expanding, tempting variety, but you can make them yourself.

Italian-style bread sticks, or *grissini*, make a good match with soups, stews, or pasta. Break apart the oversized rounds of Armenian Cracker Bread, or *lahvosh*, after they are baked and cooled to make irregular shards that invite nibbling. Herbed Sourdough Thins are seasoned, toasted slices from a long, slender loaf. Nutty Whole Wheat Squares are like savory graham crackers.

ARMENIAN CRACKER BREAD

2 eggs
1 cup milk
4 to 4½ cups flour
1½ teaspoons each sugar and salt
¼ cup vegetable shortening
4 teaspoons sesame seed

1. Preheat oven to 450° F. In a small bowl beat together eggs and milk.

2. In a large bowl mix 4 cups of the flour, the sugar, and salt. Cut in shortening until mixture resembles coarse crumbs. Gradually blend in egg mixture, mixing until dough pulls away from sides of bowl.

3. On a floured board or pastry cloth, knead dough lightly to form a smooth ball. Divide dough into 4 parts; wrap 3 of them in plastic wrap to keep them from drying out. Work with and bake one portion at a time.

4. On the floured surface, roll out dough until it is about ⅛ inch thick. Add flour as required to prevent dough from sticking. Form into a ball; then roll out again to a circle about 14 inches in diameter.

5. Transfer carefully to a greased baking sheet or pizza pan. Brush lightly with water; then sprinkle with 1 teaspoon of the sesame seed.

6. Place a shallow pan of hot water on bottom rack of oven. Place baking sheet on rack above it and bake bread for 3 minutes. Remove water, reduce heat to 300° F, and bake until bread is blistered, feels dry to the touch, and is lightly browned (12 to 15 minutes). Cool on a wire rack.

7. Repeat rolling and baking with remaining portions of dough.

8. When rounds of bread are crisp and cool, break apart to serve.

Makes 4 cracker breads, each 13 to 14 inches in diameter.

CRISP BREAD STICKS

1 envelope active dry yeast
⅔ cup warm water
¼ cup olive oil
1 teaspoon salt
1 tablespoon sugar
2¼ to 2½ cups unbleached flour
1 egg, lightly beaten with
1 teaspoon water
Sesame seed

1. In large bowl of electric mixer, sprinkle yeast over the warm water. Let stand until softened (about 5 minutes).

2. Add olive oil, salt, sugar, and 1¼ cups of the flour. Mix to blend; then beat at medium speed until smooth and elastic (about 5 minutes). Then gradually beat in about 1 cup more flour to make a stiff dough.

3. Turn dough onto a floured board or pastry cloth and knead until dough is springy and small bubbles form just beneath surface (5 to 10 minutes). Transfer to a greased bowl, cover, and leave the dough standing in a warm place until it doubles in bulk (about 1 hour).

4. Punch dough down and divide in half. Cut each half of the dough into 15 equal pieces. Using palms of hands, roll each piece on a floured surface into a stick about 12 inches long. Place about ¾ inch apart on greased baking sheets. Brush each stick lightly with egg mixture; sprinkle with sesame seed. Let rise until puffy (30 to 35 minutes).

5. Preheat oven to 325° F. Bake until golden (25 to 30 minutes). Allow bread sticks to cool on racks.

Makes 30 bread sticks.

HERBED SOURDOUGH THINS

1 sourdough baguette (15 in. long; about ½ lb)

3 tablespoons each *butter or margarine and olive oil*

1 teaspoon lemon juice

1 clove garlic, minced or pressed

½ teaspoon freeze-dried chives

¼ teaspoon each *paprika and dried savory*

½ cup grated Parmesan cheese

1. Preheat oven to 300° F. Slice the bread thinly (you should have about 48 slices). Arrange in a single layer on baking sheets.

2. In a small pan over medium heat, melt butter with oil. Add lemon juice and bring to a boil, stirring; boil for 1 minute. Mix in garlic and remove from heat. Stir in chives, paprika, and savory.

3. Brush bread slices lightly and evenly with butter mixture. Sprinkle evenly with Parmesan cheese.

4. Bake until crisp and lightly browned (30 to 35 minutes).

5. Serve hot, or let cool on wire racks and serve at room temperature. If Herbed Sourdough Thins are made more than 24 hours in advance, wrap tightly and freeze; then spread on a baking sheet and heat in a 300° F oven for about 10 minutes before serving.

Makes about 4 dozen slices.

WHOLE WHEAT SQUARES

1 egg

¾ cup milk

2 cups whole wheat flour

1 cup all-purpose flour

¼ cup wheat germ

1 teaspoon each *salt and baking powder*

6 tablespoons butter or margarine
Coarse salt

1. Preheat oven to 325° F. In a small bowl beat egg with milk. In a large bowl mix flours, wheat germ, salt, and baking powder. Cut in butter until mixture resembles coarse crumbs. Gradually blend in egg mixture, mixing until dough pulls away from sides of bowl.

2. Divide dough into 2 portions. With flour-dusted hands, flatten each portion onto a greased 12- by 15-inch baking sheet. With a floured rolling pin, roll dough out evenly to edges of pan. Using a pastry wheel or pizza cutter, mark dough into about 2-inch squares. Sprinkle with coarse salt. Pierce dough with a fork at about 1-inch intervals.

3. Bake until lightly browned (25 to 30 minutes).

4. Cool on wire racks; then carefully break apart.

Makes about 8 dozen crackers.

Any soup can benefit from a crisp home-baked accompaniment. Choose from Italian-style bread sticks, Armenian Cracker Bread, or crackers—either sourdough or whole wheat.

DRESSING UP SOUPS

No matter how good a bowl of plain soup tastes or smells, an appropriate and colorful garnish adds visual interest to entice the appetite. Adding visual interest is equally important when serving a stew, or any other meal for that matter.

An appropriate garnish must be edible, but it can be ever so simple: a mere dusting of nutmeg or freshly ground pepper, a few snips of chives or parsley, a single mushroom slice.

A puréed vegetable or creamy soup takes well to a crunchy addition such as a tiny salted pretzel, toasted hazelnuts, or the Garlic Croutons that follow.

Clear soups can be enhanced by tiny poached meatballs or Danish Meat Dumplings, or by swirls of Parsleyed Pancake Strips, as a change from noodles.

GARLIC CROUTONS

> 8 slices firm white or whole wheat bread
> 2 tablespoons each salad oil and butter
> 1 small clove garlic, minced or pressed
> 1/8 teaspoon paprika

1. Preheat oven to 350° F. Trim crusts from bread and discard them. Dice bread into 1/2-inch cubes.

2. In a large frying pan, combine oil and butter; place over medium heat until melted. Stir in garlic and paprika. Add bread. Stir until well coated.

3. Transfer bread cubes to a rimmed baking sheet and spread in a single layer. Bake until lightly browned and crisp (20 to 25 minutes). Cool; then store in a covered container in a cool place for up to 5 days.

Makes about 2½ cups.

PARSLEYED PANCAKE STRIPS

> 1 egg
> 2/3 cup milk
> 1/2 cup flour
> 1/8 teaspoon salt
> 2 tablespoons chopped parsley
> 1 to 2 tablespoons butter or margarine

1. In blender or food processor, combine egg, milk, flour, and salt. Whirl or process until batter is smooth. Stir in parsley.

2. For each pancake melt about 1/2 teaspoon of the butter in a 7- to 8-inch crepe pan or frying pan over medium heat until bubbling. Add 2 to 3 tablespoons of the batter, tilting pan so batter covers bottom evenly. Cook until pancake is set and lightly browned on each side, turning once.

3. As soon as cooked pancake is cool enough to handle, roll it up tightly. When all are cooked, cut pancake rolls into 1/8- to 1/4-inch strips.

Makes 2½ to 3 cups pancake strips.

DANISH MEAT DUMPLINGS

> 1/2 pound cubed lean pork shoulder
> 1/4 cup coarsely chopped onion
> 3 tablespoons flour
> 1/2 teaspoon salt
>   Pinch each white pepper and ground nutmeg
> 1 egg white
> 1/4 to 1/3 cup milk
> 8 cups salted water

1. In food processor with metal blade, combine pork, onion, flour, salt, pepper, nutmeg, and egg white. Process until pork is very finely chopped. Then add milk through feed tube, a little at a time, until mixture has consistency of cooked oatmeal.

2. In a 3-quart pan bring the salted water to a boil. Drop about half of the meat mixture by rounded teaspoons into the water. As soon as the water returns to a boil, add a little cold water. Bring to a boil again, add a little more cold water to slow boiling, and repeat this process once more. Remove dumplings with a slotted spoon and drain well. Repeat with remaining meat mixture.

3. If dumplings are made ahead of time, arrange them in a shallow pan in a single layer; cover, and refrigerate for up to 1 day. Add them to hot soup to reheat.

Makes about 3 dozen small dumplings.

HERBS, VEGETABLES, AND FLOWERS

While it's true that the proof of the pudding is in the eating, the presentation of a dish is just as important as the aroma when it comes to whetting the appetite.

When garnishing, the only rule you need obey is that whatever is used should be edible. Chopped herbs, herb sprigs, a leaf or two, citrus peel, pieces of vegetables and fruits carved into attractive shapes, edible flowers, seeds, nuts—all are acceptable. In fact, not only are unusual and creative garnishes acceptable, the popularity of nouvelle cuisine (which relies heavily on presentation) has made it fashionable to decorate and dress up a meal.

Herbs can be kept in the freezer for up to a year. Wash them in cold water after removing any deteriorating leaves. Pat them completely dry with paper towels, then package in small, airtight bags.

Meat marinates in red wine for as much as a day before it is simmered to become an elegant Cocotte of Beef, Mushrooms, and Wine (see page 80).

Savory Meat Stews

Many of the world's great dishes are stews—meat cooked slowly in a well-seasoned liquid until it is tender, moist, and irresistible. Every country has at least one stew that could be considered a national dish—indeed, a national treasure. Italy gives us *bollito misto* (see page 82); Belgium, *carbonnade* (see page 83); and Germany, *sauerbraten* (see page 96). In the southwestern United States, chili is the stew cooks strive to perfect (see pages 88-89). Most of these stews require a fair amount of cooking time. But once you have them safely simmering, you can usually ignore them while you attend to other matters.

BEEF STEWS

These substantial stews also have a certain finesse. Many call for inexpensive cuts of meat so, when you serve one for a dinner party, you are investing more time than money.

COCOTTE OF BEEF, MUSHROOMS, AND WINE

The capacious saucepan in which this stew simmers gives the dish its name.

- 3 pounds lean beef (chuck or rump), cut in 1-inch cubes
- ¼ cup brandy
- 2 tablespoons olive oil
- 2 medium onions, thinly slivered
- 2 cloves garlic, minced or pressed
- 1 teaspoon salt
- ½ teaspoon each sugar, peppercorns, juniper berries, and dried thyme
- ⅛ teaspoon each whole cloves and ground nutmeg
- 1 bay leaf
- 1½ cups dry red wine
- 3 tablespoons butter or margarine
- ½ pound large mushrooms, quartered
- 1 cup Sturdy Beef Broth (see page 8) or canned regular-strength beef broth
- 1 tablespoon tomato paste
- 1 tablespoon cornstarch, blended with 2 tablespoons beef broth or water
- Chopped parsley, for garnish

1. Place cubed beef in a large, deep bowl; mix lightly with brandy and 1 tablespoon of the oil. Add onions, garlic, salt, sugar, peppercorns, juniper berries, thyme, cloves, nutmeg, and bay leaf. Pour in wine, mixing beef lightly with seasonings. Cover and refrigerate for 8 to 24 hours. Remove beef and onions from marinade; reserve marinade; pat beef dry.

2. In a heavy 4- to 5-quart saucepan, heat remaining 1 tablespoon oil with butter over medium heat. Add mushrooms; cook until browned; remove.

3. In same pan brown beef cubes well in batches, removing them as they brown. Add onions; cook until limp. Return beef and mushrooms to pan. Add broth and tomato paste. Strain marinade; discard seasonings; add marinade to pan. Bring to a boil, cover, reduce heat, and simmer until meat is very tender (2 to 2½ hours).

4. Using a slotted spoon, remove beef and mushrooms to a warm serving dish and keep warm. Skim and discard fat from cooking liquid. Bring liquid to a boil over high heat, stirring, and cook until it is reduced by about a fourth. Remove from heat and blend in cornstarch mixture. Cook, stirring often, until thickened and clear. Taste; add salt if needed.

5. Pour sauce over beef and mushrooms. Garnish with parsley.

Serves 6.

BRAISED SHORT RIBS WITH PEPPERS

Here is another savory beef dish of Italian origin. Red and green bell peppers give the abundant sauce substance and also act as a colorful garnish in the finished dish.

- 3½ to 4 pounds English-cut beef short ribs, cut in serving pieces
- Salt and coarsely ground pepper
- 2 tablespoons each butter or margarine and olive oil
- 2 large onions
- 2 teaspoons dried basil
- ½ teaspoon dried rosemary
- 1 medium carrot, shredded
- 1 stalk celery, finely chopped
- 2 each red and green bell peppers
- 1 large clove garlic, minced or pressed
- 1 can (8 oz) tomato sauce
- 1 cup dry red wine
- 3 tablespoons rum (optional)

1. Sprinkle short ribs with salt and pepper. In a large, deep frying pan or Dutch oven over medium heat, melt 1 tablespoon of the butter with 1 tablespoon of the olive oil. Add ribs, about half at a time, and brown on all sides. Remove ribs as they brown.

2. After ribs are browned, spoon off all but about 2 tablespoons of the drippings. To same pan add 1 of the onions (chopped), 1 teaspoon of the basil, ¼ teaspoon of the rosemary, the carrot, and the celery. Remove seeds from bell peppers and chop 1 red and 1 green pepper; add to onion mixture in pan. Cook, stirring, until onions are soft but not browned. Mix in garlic.

3. Return browned short ribs to pan. Blend in tomato sauce and wine. Bring to a boil, cover, reduce heat, and simmer until short ribs are very tender (2½ to 3 hours).

4. About 20 minutes before short ribs finish cooking, thinly sliver remaining onion and peppers. In a large frying pan, heat remaining 1 tablespoon each olive oil and butter over moderate heat. Add onion and cook, stirring often, until limp. Mix in peppers and remaining basil and rosemary. Continue cooking until onions brown lightly and peppers are tender-crisp (10 to 12 minutes). Remove from heat and keep warm.

5. Remove short ribs to a warm, deep platter and cover lightly to keep warm. Skim and discard fat from liquid in which short ribs cooked. Purée cooking liquid in blender or food processor; then add rum (if used) and reheat to serve. Taste, and add salt if needed. Pour on sauce; then spoon sautéed onion-and-pepper mixture over and around ribs.

Serves 8.

TANGY POT ROAST STEW

When people talk about the wonders of mother's (or grandmother's) cooking, the conversation usually comes around to pot roast. If your mother comes from the region of Emilia-Romagna in Italy, perhaps this is the way she cooks it.

- 2 tablespoons olive oil
- 1 blade-cut or seven-bone chuck roast (3½ to 4 lbs), fat trimmed
- 2 red onions, slivered
- 1 package (12 oz) fresh baby carrots, scrubbed and trimmed (unpeeled)
- 1 stalk celery, thinly sliced
- 2 cloves garlic, minced or pressed
- 1 teaspoon salt
- ¼ teaspoon each ground cloves and coarsely ground pepper
- ½ teaspoon dried thyme
- 1 cup Sturdy Beef Broth (see page 8) or canned regular-strength beef broth
- 2 tablespoons balsamic vinegar or red wine vinegar
  Chopped parsley, for garnish

1. In a large, deep frying pan over medium heat or an electric frying pan on medium setting, heat oil. Add roast and brown well on all sides; remove and reserve roast. Spoon off and discard all but about 2 tablespoons of the drippings. Add onions, carrots, and celery, and cook, stirring, until onions are browned lightly. Mix in garlic.

2. Sprinkle both sides of browned roast with mixture of salt, cloves, pepper, and thyme. Place roast on top of vegetables in pan. Pour broth over roast; drizzle with vinegar. Cover, reduce heat, and simmer until meat is very tender (2½ to 3 hours).

3. Remove roast to a warm platter or board. Remove and discard bones, dividing roast into several large sections. Slice each section across the grain. Arrange vegetables around roast. Cover with foil to keep warm.

4. Skim and discard surface fat from cooking liquid. Bring to a boil, stirring, until it is reduced and slightly thickened. Sprinkle pot roast with chopped parsley and serve with sauce.

Serves 4 to 6.

VIENNESE SIMMERED DINNER

For this presentation, choose the cone-shaped muscle of the blade chuck, which when separated out as a roast, is called chuck tender, mock tender, Scotch tender, or Jewish fillet. If this small boneless roast is not available, use brisket.

This recipe produces a creamy first-course soup and a main dish of sliced beef with horseradish sauce.

- 1 chuck fillet roast or fresh brisket (3 lbs)
- 6 cups water
- 2 leeks
- 3 medium carrots, thinly sliced
- 1 medium parsnip or turnip, peeled and finely chopped
- 1 small celery root (½ to ¾ lb), peeled and finely chopped
- 1 small onion, finely chopped
- 1 teaspoon salt
- ⅛ teaspoon white pepper
- 3 sprigs parsley
- 6 small new potatoes (1 to 1¼ lbs)
- ⅛ teaspoon paprika
- ½ cup whipping cream
  Finely chopped parsley, for garnish
  Sour pickles and sharp mustard

Horseradish Cream Sauce

- ½ cup whipping cream
- ¼ teaspoon each sugar and dry mustard
- ½ teaspoon lemon juice
- 2 tablespoons prepared horseradish

1. Preheat oven to 500° F. Place beef in a shallow roasting pan. Bake, uncovered, turning once, until well browned (15 to 20 minutes). Transfer to a 5½- to 6-quart kettle. Add a little of the water to roasting pan, stirring to loosen drippings. Pour over roast.

2. Cut off root ends of leeks; remove and discard coarse outer leaves. Cut off and discard green tops. Split lengthwise, from leafy end, cutting to within about 1 inch of root end. Soak in cold water for several minutes; then separate leaves under running water to rinse away any clinging grit; drain. Slice about ¼ inch thick.

3. To kettle add leeks, carrots, parsnip, celery root, onion, salt, pepper, parsley, and remaining water. Bring to a boil, cover, reduce heat, and simmer for 2½ hours.

4. Prepare Horseradish Cream Sauce.

5. To kettle add potatoes; continue cooking until beef is very tender (30 minutes to 1 hour). Remove meat and potatoes from kettle and reserve.

6. Strain broth, reserving vegetables. Measure 3 cups of the broth and return remainder to kettle over low heat. Return beef and potatoes to broth, cover, and keep warm until ready to serve.

7. In blender or food processor, combine the 3 cups broth and reserved vegetables from broth (about half of each at a time). Whirl or process until smooth. Transfer to a 2½- to 3-quart saucepan and blend in paprika and cream. Stir over medium heat until soup is steaming hot. Taste, and add salt and white pepper if needed. Serve as a first-course soup.

8. Then arrange warm beef and potatoes on a board or warm platter. Slice beef thinly across the grain to serve. Drizzle with a little of the remaining broth. Sprinkle with parsley and accompany with Horseradish Cream Sauce, pickles, and mustard. Freeze remaining broth.

Serves 6.

Horseradish Cream Sauce In a medium bowl combine cream, sugar, mustard, and lemon juice. Beat until stiff. Fold in horseradish. Cover and refrigerate for 1 to 3 hours.

Makes about 1 cup.

1 large onion, finely chopped
4 large carrots
2 stalks celery, sliced
5 sprigs parsley
1 tablespoons salt
¼ teaspoon each *whole allspice and black peppercorns*
1 *coteghino* sausage (1 to 1½ lbs; optional)
4 to 6 leeks, well rinsed, with coarse outer leaves discarded and leafy tops trimmed to about 5 inches
10 to 12 small red potatoes, scrubbed (unpeeled)
1 small Savoy (curly) cabbage (about 1 lb), cut into 8 wedges

Green Sauce

½ cup olive oil
¼ cup white wine vinegar
3 green onions, coarsely chopped
1 cup lightly packed parsley sprigs
2 tablespoons capers
1 clove garlic, minced or pressed
1 tablespoon anchovy paste
Pinch pepper
¼ cup lightly packed fresh basil leaves or 1 tablespoon dried basil
Salt (optional)

1. Preheat oven to 500° F. Place roast in a shallow roasting pan. Bake, uncovered, turning once, until well browned (20 to 25 minutes). Transfer to a 10- to 12-quart kettle. Add a little of the water to pan, stirring to loosen brown drippings; pour over roast.

2. To kettle add tongue, veal shank, and onion. Slice 1 of the carrots and add it to meats with celery, parsley, salt, allspice, peppercorns, and remaining water. Bring to a boil over medium heat, cover, reduce heat, and simmer for 2 hours. Add sausage (if used), cover again, and cook for 1 hour more until meats are tender.

A piquant green sauce unites all elements in Boiled Dinner Bolognese. If you wish, serve the cooking broth as a first course. Or, strain and freeze it to use later as the base for your next bollito misto.

BOILED DINNER BOLOGNESE

A dazzling array of meats and vegetables, each added at just the right stage to achieve tenderness, makes up the Italian simmered dinner known as *bollito misto*.

Look for the distinctive, plump *coteghino* sausage in Italian delicatessens; if it isn't stocked regularly, perhaps the dealer can order it for you. It contributes a lot of flavor to the dish.

1 beef rump roast (3½ to 4 lbs)
12 cups water or Sturdy Beef Broth (see page 8)
1 fresh beef tongue (2½ to 3 lbs)
1 veal shank (1 to 1½ lbs), cut through bone into 3 sections

3. Meanwhile, cut 3 remaining carrots lengthwise into quarters; cut quarters crosswise into halves. Add to kettle with leeks and potatoes; cook until meats and potatoes are tender (about 45 minutes).

4. With a slotted spoon remove tongue and set it aside. Remove roast, veal shank, and sausage to a large, warm platter. Surround with leeks, potatoes, and carrots. Cover lightly with foil and keep warm.

5. Cut off and discard bones and gristle at the thick end of the tongue. Slit the skin on the underside, and starting at the thick end, peel it off. Add tongue to meats and vegetables on platter.

6. Add cabbage to gently boiling broth and cook, uncovered, until it is tender and bright green (8 to 10 minutes). Add to meats and vegetables on platter.

7. While cabbage cooks, prepare Green Sauce.

8. If you wish to serve broth as a first course, strain, salt if needed, and serve it hot.

9. Then carve meats and serve with vegetables and Green Sauce.

Serves 10 to 12.

Green Sauce In a blender or food processor combine olive oil, vinegar, onion, parsley, capers, garlic, anchovy paste, pepper, and basil. Whirl or process until smoothly blended. Taste, and add salt if needed. Serve at room temperature.

Makes about 1¼ cups.

FLEMISH BEEF IN BEER

In the traditional Belgian *carbonnade*, beer is the choice for cooking beef to tenderness. This stew calls for simmering a rump roast in the oven.

   1 *boneless rump roast (4 to 5 lbs)*
   1 *tablespoon each butter or margarine and salad oil*
   1 *teaspoon salt*
  ¼ *teaspoon ground pepper*
  ¾ *teaspoon dried rosemary*
   1 *pound small white boiling onions, peeled*
   2 *tablespoons red wine vinegar*
   1 *tablespoon tomato paste*
   1 *clove garlic, minced or pressed*
   2 *bottles (12 oz each) dark beer*
   2 *teaspoons Dijon mustard*
   1 *tablespoon flour, creamed with 1 tablespoon soft butter*
      Additional vinegar (optional)
      Chopped parsley, for garnish

1. Preheat oven to 350° F. In a large frying pan over medium-high heat, heat butter and oil. Add roast and brown on all sides.

2. Reserving frying pan, place roast in a deep 3- to 5-quart covered casserole. Sprinkle with salt, pepper, and rosemary. Surround with onions. Combine vinegar, tomato paste, and garlic and drizzle over onions. Discard fat from frying pan. Add a little of the beer and stir to dissolve brown drippings. Add drippings to casserole with remaining beer.

3. Bake until meat is very tender (4 to 4½ hours).

4. Spoon or pour cooking liquid into a large, deep frying pan. Keep meat and onions warm in casserole in turned-off oven. Bring liquid to a boil; then blend in first mustard, then bits of flour mixture, stirring until sauce is thickened. Taste, and add more vinegar if needed.

5. Slice meat thinly and arrange it on a warm, rimmed platter with onions around it. Spoon sauce over. Sprinkle with parsley.

Serves 8 to 10.

GRANDMOTHER'S BRAISED ROUND STEAK

Serve this with fusilli or penne to catch the rich sauce in every swirl.

   1 *full-cut round steak, boneless or bone-in (2 lbs), fat trimmed*
      Salt and pepper
   1 *tablespoon each butter or margarine and olive oil*
   2 *large shallots, finely chopped (about ⅓ cup)*
   1 *medium carrot, finely grated*
   1 *large clove garlic, minced or pressed*
  ¾ *teaspoon dried basil*
  ½ *teaspoon dried oregano*
  ¼ *teaspoon dried rosemary, crumbled*
   1 *tablespoon Worcestershire sauce*
   1 *can (8 oz) tomato sauce*
  ½ *cup dry red wine*
      Up to ½ cup additional red wine

1. Lightly sprinkle round steak on both sides with salt and pepper. In a large, heavy frying pan over medium-high heat, melt butter with oil. Add round steak (in one piece) and brown well on both sides.

2. When second side is nearly browned, add shallots and carrot around steak; stir and brown lightly. Add garlic, basil, oregano, rosemary, and Worcestershire sauce. Mix in tomato sauce and the ½ cup wine.

3. Bring to a boil, cover, reduce heat, and simmer until round steak is very tender (1¼ to 1½ hours).

4. Remove round steak to a warm platter and keep warm. If necessary, skim and discard surface fat from cooking liquid. Bring sauce to a boil, stirring and adding more wine if it is too thick. Taste; add salt if needed.

5. Divide round steak into serving pieces. Pour sauce over it.

Serves 6.

FAMILY FAVORITE DINNER

Creamy Meatball Stroganoff

Noodles

Crisp Coleslaw

Warm Espresso Brownies With Ice Cream

Milk

Red Jug Wine

Coffee

For this dinner, make the coleslaw first so that it can chill to crisp and blend flavors while you are preparing the meatballs. If you put the rich, extra-chocolatey brownies into the oven to bake while you are enjoying the main dish, they will be ready to cut and serve warm for dessert.

CREAMY MEATBALL STROGANOFF

2 tablespoons butter or margarine
1 tablespoon salad oil
1 medium onion, thinly slivered
½ pound mushrooms, sliced
1 clove garlic, minced or pressed
¼ teaspoon paprika
1 teaspoon Worcestershire sauce
½ cup Sturdy Beef Broth (see page 8) or canned regular-strength beef broth
2 teaspoons cornstarch, blended with 1 tablespoon water
½ cup sour cream
Cooked noodles
Chopped parsley, for garnish

Stroganoff Meatballs

1 egg
¼ cup milk
¾ cup soft bread crumbs
1 teaspoon salt
⅛ teaspoon each ground ginger and ground nutmeg
1 teaspoon Worcestershire sauce
1 pound ground lean beef
½ pound ground lean pork, veal, or turkey

1. Prepare Stroganoff Meatballs. In a large, heavy frying pan over medium heat, melt butter with oil. Add meatballs, about half at a time, and cook until browned, removing them to a shallow pan. When all meatballs are browned, place pan of them (uncovered) in a 250° F oven while you prepare the sauce. Pour off and discard all but about 2 tablespoons of the drippings in the frying pan (if necessary).

2. To the frying pan add onion and mushrooms; cook, stirring, until both are lightly browned and most of the mushroom liquid has cooked away. Mix in garlic, paprika, Worcestershire sauce, and broth, stirring to blend in brown bits from pan. Stir in cornstarch mixture, mixing until thickened and smooth.

3. Add meatballs to mushroom sauce, cover, reduce heat, and simmer for 10 minutes. Remove from heat and blend in sour cream, stirring carefully to avoid breaking the meatballs. Return to low heat, stirring occasionally, until sauce is just heated through. Taste, and add salt if needed.

4. Serve over noodles; sprinkle with parsley.

Serves 4 to 6.

Stroganoff Meatballs In a large bowl beat egg with milk. Blend in bread crumbs, salt, ginger, nutmeg, and Worcestershire sauce. Add ground meats, mix lightly. Then shape in 1-inch balls.

CRISP COLESLAW

1 small green cabbage (1 to 1¼ lbs), thinly shredded (about 8 cups)
1 red or green bell pepper, seeded and thinly slivered
½ cup each finely chopped parsley and thinly sliced green onions
1½ tablespoons sugar
1½ teaspoons salt
¼ teaspoon dry mustard
½ cup distilled white vinegar
⅓ cup olive oil

1. In a large bowl mix cabbage, bell pepper, parsley, and green onions.

2. For dressing, shake (in a covered jar) or stir together sugar, salt, dry mustard, vinegar, and oil until sugar dissolves.

3. Pour dressing over cabbage mixture; mix lightly. Cover and refrigerate until salad is well chilled and flavors are blended (30 minutes to 3 hours).

Serves 6.

ESPRESSO BROWNIES

- 3 squares (3 oz) unsweetened chocolate
- ½ cup butter or margarine
- 1 teaspoon instant coffee powder or granules
- ⅔ cup flour
- ½ teaspoon baking powder
- ¼ teaspoon salt
- 2 eggs
- ½ cup each granulated sugar and firmly packed brown sugar
- 1 teaspoon vanilla extract
- ½ cup chopped walnuts
  Confectioners' sugar, for dusting tops
  Ice cream (optional)

1. Preheat oven to 350° F. In a small pan over low heat, combine chocolate, butter, and instant coffee. When butter is melted and chocolate is shiny, stir well to blend together.

2. In a small bowl stir together flour, baking powder, and salt.

3. In a large bowl, beat eggs until thick; gradually beat in sugars until they are well combined. Blend in chocolate mixture, then vanilla. Gradually stir in flour mixture and mix until all ingredients are well blended. Fold in walnuts.

4. Spread in a greased, lightly floured 8-inch square pan. Bake until edges begin to pull away from sides of pan and center is nearly set when tested with a wooden pick (25 to 30 minutes; do not overbake).

5. Let cool in pan on a wire rack for a few minutes; then cut into bars. Sift confectioners' sugar over brownies.

6. Serve with ice cream on the side.
Makes 18 brownies.

Meatballs in a creamy sauce served over noodles are the main course for a quick family dinner. Cole-slaw and homemade brownies with ice cream complete the meal.

INDIVIDUAL POT ROASTS

When you cook plump beef shanks with such traditional vegetables as carrots, mushrooms, and onions in a rich red-brown sauce, they are transformed into one-to-a-person pot roasts in about two hours' time.

    4   beef shank slices, about 1 inch
        thick (about 2½ lbs in all)
        Salt, pepper, and flour
    2   tablespoons butter or
        margarine
    1   tablespoon salad oil
    1   large onion, thinly slivered
    1   stalk celery, thinly sliced
    ½   pound mushrooms, quartered
        (leave whole if small)
    2   cloves garlic, minced or
        pressed
    3   medium carrots, cut length-
        wise in quarters, then in
        2-inch-long sticks
    8   small white boiling onions
        (optional)
    1   bay leaf
    ¼   teaspoon dried thyme
    1   can (1 lb) tomatoes
    ½   cup dry red wine
    1   tablespoon flour
        Chopped parsley, for garnish

1. Sprinkle beef shanks on all sides with salt and pepper; then coat lightly with flour. Place 1 tablespoon of the butter in a small bowl and set aside to soften. In a large, deep, heavy frying pan over medium-high heat, melt remaining butter with oil. Add beef shanks and brown well on all sides, removing them from pan as they brown.

2. To drippings in pan add slivered onion, celery, and mushrooms. Cook, stirring often, until onion is soft and mushrooms brown lightly. Mix in garlic, carrots, boiling onions (if used), bay leaf, and thyme. Return beef shanks to pan.

3. Add tomatoes (coarsely chopped) and their liquid and wine. Bring to a boil, cover, reduce heat, and simmer until meat is very tender (2 to 2½ hours). Meanwhile, blend the 1 tablespoon flour smoothly with the reserved 1 tablespoon butter.

4. Using a slotted spatula, remove beef shanks and vegetables carefully to a warm serving dish. If necessary, skim and discard surface fat from cooking liquid. Bring liquid to a boil over high heat, stirring in brown bits from pan. Add flour mixture, a little at a time, stirring until sauce thickens and boils. Taste, and add salt if needed.

5. Pour sauce over beef shanks and sprinkle with parsley to serve.

Serves 4.

SMOTHERED SKIRT STEAKS

The skirt steak is a rather obscure bit of beef. It lies inside the rib cage, and there are only two to a carcass. For unique texture and flavor, it is worth searching out. You may have to ask for it, because in many markets, this is "the steak the butcher takes home."

    4   skirt steaks, about 1 inch thick
        (about 1½ lbs in all)
        Salt, pepper, and paprika
    1½ tablespoons butter or
        margarine
    1   tablespoon salad oil
    1   medium onion, slivered
    ½   pound mushrooms, quartered
        (leave whole if small)
    1   clove garlic, minced or pressed
    2   medium carrots, cut length-
        wise in quarters, then thinly
        sliced
    ½   teaspoon dried savory
    2   teaspoons Dijon mustard
    ⅓   cup each dry red wine and
        Sturdy Beef Broth (see page 8)
        or canned regular-strength
        beef broth
    2   teaspoons flour
        Chopped parsley, for garnish

1. Sprinkle steaks on all sides with salt, pepper, and paprika. Place ½ tablespoon of the butter in a small bowl and set aside to soften. In a large, heavy frying pan over medium-high heat, melt remaining 1 tablespoon butter with oil. Add steaks and brown well on all sides, removing them as they brown. Reduce heat to medium.

2. Spoon off and discard all but about 2 tablespoons of the drippings (if necessary). Add onion and mushrooms. Cook, stirring often, until onion is soft, mushrooms have browned lightly, and most of the mushroom liquid has cooked away. Mix in garlic, carrots, savory, and mustard.

3. Return steaks to pan. Pour in wine and broth. Bring to a boil, cover, reduce heat, and simmer until steaks and vegetables are tender (30 to 45 minutes). Meanwhile, blend flour smoothly with the reserved ½ tablespoon butter.

4. Remove steaks to a warm platter and keep them warm. Bring cooking liquid to a boil over high heat, stirring often. Add flour mixture, bit by bit, stirring until sauce is thickened. Taste, and add salt if needed. Spoon sauce over steaks.

5. Serve sprinkled with parsley.

Serves 4.

FLANK STEAK STIFADO

Stifado is a Greek stew to which most cooks would devote hours. But if made with flank steak, as this speedy stew is, it cooks in minutes. The seasonings consist of sweet-sour accents, spices, oregano, and an abundance of onions.

A last-minute topping of crumbled feta cheese melts over the hot steak strips as you bring the dish to the table. Accompany it with a ring of sesame bread, a green vegetable or carrots, and red wine or retsina.

> 1 to 1½ *pounds flank steak*
>   *Salt and pepper*
> ¼ *teaspoon each* ground cinnamon *and dried* oregano
> ⅛ *teaspoon each* ground ginger *and* ground allspice
> 2 *tablespoons butter or margarine*
> 1 *tablespoon olive oil*
> 1 *medium onion, thinly slivered*
> 1 *large clove garlic, minced or pressed*
> 1 *tablespoon each* brown sugar, tomato paste, *and* red wine vinegar
> ½ *cup dry red wine*
> ⅓ *cup crumbled feta cheese*
>   *Sprigs of Italian (flat-leaf) parsley, for garnish*

1. Cut steak across the grain, slicing on the diagonal (if this is difficult, partially freeze the meat first) to make thin strips about 1 inch wide and 2 inches long. Sprinkle with salt and pepper. In a small bowl mix cinnamon, oregano, ginger, and allspice; sprinkle mixture evenly over all sides of steak strips.

2. In a large, deep, heavy frying pan over medium-high heat, melt butter with oil. Add steak strips and brown on all sides, a half to a third at a time. (The important thing is *not* to crowd the pan, so that steak can brown quickly without giving up any moisture.) Remove strips of steak as soon as they are brown.

3. When all the meat is browned and out of the pan, reduce heat to medium and add onion. Cook, stirring often, until soft and lightly browned. Blend in garlic, then brown sugar, tomato paste, and vinegar. Add wine. Bring to a boil, cover, reduce heat, and cook for 15 minutes.

4. Increase heat to medium, and cook and stir onion mixture, uncovered, until it is slightly reduced and thickened. Mix in beef strips and any juices that collected as the beef stood; turn meat gently, coating with onion mixture, until meat is heated through. Taste, and add salt if needed.

5. Transfer to a warm, shallow casserole, and sprinkle with cheese and parsley. Serve at once.

Serves 4 to 6.

Crumbled feta cheese serves as both a garnish and a taste accent. The special tang is an appropriate flavor for a Greek Flank Steak Stifado.

Tequila and orange rind and juice flavor this all-meat version of that perennial favorite—chili. Serve it from the skillet if you like, dressing up each serving with a dollop of sour cream, cilantro, and sliced avocados.

SOME LIKE IT HOT: CHILIS

For chili fanciers, here are three recipes to broaden your scope.

ALL-MEAT VEAL CHILI

There are no beans in this first version of chili.

½ pound *mild Italian sausages*
1 pound *ground veal or ground turkey, crumbled*
1 *orange*
1 *medium onion, finely chopped*
1 *red or green bell pepper, seeded and chopped*
1 *clove garlic, minced or pressed*
1 teaspoon *each salt and paprika*
¾ teaspoon *ground cumin*
⅛ teaspoon *ground cloves*
1 *small dried hot red chile, crushed*
1 can (1 lb) *tomatoes*
¼ cup *tomato paste*
½ cup *tequila*
   Sour cream, cilantro (Chinese parsley) sprigs, and avocado slices, for garnish

1. Remove casings from sausages; crumble meat into a large, deep, heavy frying pan. Cook over medium-high heat, stirring often, until lightly browned. Mix in ground veal and cook until it begins to brown. Meanwhile, grate rind and squeeze juice from orange; reserve both.

2. To meats add onion and bell pepper. Cook over medium heat, stirring often, until onion is soft and lightly browned. Mix in garlic, salt, paprika, cumin, cloves, and chile. Stir in orange rind and juice, tomatoes (coarsely chopped), tomato liquid, tomato paste, and tequila. Bring to a boil, cover, reduce heat, and simmer about 1 hour.

3. If chili is soupy, uncover and cook over medium-low heat, stirring occasionally. Taste; add salt if needed.

4. Serve garnished with sour cream, cilantro, and avocado slices.

Serves 4.

PINTO BEAN CHILI

This beef and pinto bean chili may strike you as the most traditional version.

- 1 cup dried pinto beans, rinsed and drained
- 3 cups water
- 2 tablespoons butter or margarine
- 2 pounds boneless beef chuck, fat trimmed, cut in 1-inch cubes
- 1 large onion, finely chopped
- 1 clove garlic, minced or pressed
- 2 teaspoons salt
- 1 teaspoon ground cumin
- 1 tablespoon chili powder
- 1 can (1 lb) tomatoes
- 1 can (4 oz) diced green chiles
- 1 can (8 oz) tomato sauce
  Shredded Cheddar cheese (optional)

1. In a large, heavy saucepan, bring beans and the water to a boil. Boil briskly for 2 minutes; then remove from heat, cover, and let stand for 1 hour.

2. In a large, deep frying pan or Dutch oven over medium-high heat, melt butter. Add beef cubes, about half at a time, and brown well on all sides, removing and reserving meat as it browns. When all the beef is removed from pan, add onion to pan and cook, stirring often, until soft and lightly browned. Return beef to pan. Mix in garlic, beans and their liquid, salt, cumin, chili powder, tomatoes (coarsely chopped) and their liquid, and green chiles.

3. Bring to a boil, cover, reduce heat, and simmer until beef and beans are tender (2 to 2½ hours).

4. Mix in tomato sauce and cook, uncovered, stirring occasionally, until chili is thickened to your taste (about 15 minutes).

5. Serve bowls of hot chili with cheese to sprinkle over, if you wish.

Serves 6 to 8.

BAKED BLACK BEAN CHILI

A third chili recipe is an oven version with beans, pork and beef, and a topping of Monterey jack cheese.

- 1 cup dried black beans, rinsed and drained
- 2½ cups water
- 2 tablespoons flour
- 1 tablespoon paprika
- ¼ teaspoon cayenne pepper
- 1½ teaspoons salt
- 1 teaspoon ground cumin
- ½ teaspoon dried oregano
- 1 pound boneless beef stew meat, cut in 1-inch cubes
- 2 pounds lean boneless pork butt, cut in 1-inch cubes
- 1 tablespoon lard or soft shortening
- 1 large onion, finely chopped
- 2 cloves garlic, minced or pressed
- 1 can (4 oz) diced green chiles
- 1 can (1 lb) tomatoes
- 2 tablespoons tomato paste
  Shredded jack cheese, for garnish

1. In a large, heavy saucepan, bring beans and water to a boil. Boil for 2 minutes; then remove from heat and let stand, covered, for 1 hour.

2. Preheat oven to 375° F. In a large bowl blend flour, paprika, cayenne, salt, cumin, and oregano. Add cubed meats and mix lightly to coat with flour mixture. Place half of the meat in a deep 4- to 5-quart casserole.

3. In a medium frying pan over medium heat, melt lard. Add onion and cook until soft and beginning to brown. Mix in garlic; spoon over meats in casserole. Add green chiles, beans and water in which they soaked, tomatoes (coarsely chopped) and their liquid, and tomato paste. Top with remaining meat.

4. Cover and bake until beef and beans are tender and sauce thickens (3 to 3½ hours), stirring once after about 2 hours.

5. Stir well; add salt if needed. Serve sprinkled with jack cheese.

Serves 6 to 8.

DRYING CHILE PEPPERS

A string of dried chile peppers will ensure that you are never caught without this spicy ingredient as well as providing you with an interesting and colorful decorative addition to your kitchen decor.

Green and reddish Anaheim peppers and yellow, green, or orange jalapeño peppers can all be dried successfully.

Drying at Room Temperature
Thread a trussing needle with kitchen string, nylon thread, or fishing line and push the needle through the stem of each chile. Position chiles alternately to the left and right. Tie a loop at the top of the string. Hang chiles in a warm, dry place for about three weeks, until they shrivel and feel dry. Be warned that high humidity can cause peppers to spoil before they dry.

Drying in a Dehydrator, Oven, or the Sun *Whole, halved, or sliced chile peppers or whole peppers on a string will dry in 2 to 5 hours in a 140° F oven, and in 12 to 18 hours in a dehydrator set at 120° F. Chiles will take one or two days to dry in the sunshine.*

VEAL STEWS

Veal breast is often stuffed whole, then braised in liquid or roasted. It's a memorable entrée, but it takes a long time to get ready and to cook. For speedier preparation, have the butcher cut through the breastbone in several places so that you can separate the meat into single-rib sections.

VEAL BREAST BRAISED IN SOAVE

Accompany the stew with quickly cooked spinach or chard.

- 1 breast of veal (2½ to 3 lbs), cut in serving pieces
  Salt and white pepper
- 2 to 4 tablespoons olive oil
- 1 medium onion, slivered
- 1 medium carrot, shredded
- 1 clove garlic, minced or pressed
- ½ teaspoon dried sage
- ¾ cup each Soave or other dry white wine and Sturdy Beef Broth or Rich Chicken Broth (see page 8) or canned broth
- ¼ cup chopped parsley

1. Sprinkle pieces of veal on all sides with salt and pepper. In a large, heavy frying pan or Dutch oven, heat 2 tablespoons of the oil over moderate heat. Add veal, about half at a time, and brown on all sides, adding more oil as needed. Remove and reserve pieces as they brown.

2. To same pan add onion and carrot and cook, stirring often, until onion is soft and lightly browned. Mix in garlic and sage. Return veal to pan. Pour in wine and broth.

3. Bring to a boil, cover, reduce heat, and simmer until veal is very tender (about 1½ hours). Remove veal to a serving dish and keep warm.

4. Increase heat to high and bring liquid in pan to a boil, stirring often. Cook until liquid begins to thicken and looks syrupy. Stir in parsley. Taste, and add salt if needed. Pour sauce over veal.

Serves 4.

LEMONY VEAL AND SPINACH

This distinctive veal stew is a variation of a recipe Rosemary Hinton Barron teaches at her Kandra Kitchen cooking school on the island of Santorini. The stew cooks in just a little more than an hour.

- 2 pounds boneless veal shoulder, cut in 1-inch cubes
  Salt and white pepper
- 2 to 3 tablespoons olive oil
- 2 medium onions, thinly slivered
- 1½ teaspoons ground cumin
- 1 cup Rich Chicken Broth (see page 8) or canned chicken broth
- 1 bunch (about 12 oz) spinach
- 1 egg
- 3 tablespoons lemon juice

1. Sprinkle veal with salt and pepper. In a large, deep, heavy frying pan or Dutch oven, heat 2 tablespoons of the oil over medium heat. Add veal, about half at a time; brown lightly on all sides. Remove from pan as it browns.

2. Add onions to same pan; cook, stirring often, until soft but not browned. Mix in cumin. Return veal to pan. Add broth, bring to a boil, cover, reduce heat, and simmer until veal is tender (1 to 1¼ hours).

3. Meanwhile, remove and discard stems from spinach. Wash, pat dry, and cut leaves crosswise in 1-inch-wide strips; reserve.

4. When veal is tender, uncover and cook for about 10 minutes to reduce cooking liquid slightly. Stir in spinach. Cook over medium-low heat, stirring occasionally, until spinach is wilted and bright green.

5. In a medium bowl beat egg with lemon juice. Spoon off about ¼ cup of the veal cooking liquid; whisk hot liquid into egg mixture. Then, off heat, gradually blend egg mixture into veal stew. Return to low heat and cook, stirring gently, until stew is thickened and heated through. *Do not boil.* Taste, and add salt if needed. Serve at once.

Serves 6.

SWISS VEAL SHANKS IN WHITE WINE CREAM

Toss noodles with butter and a little grated Parmesan cheese to serve with these creamy veal shanks.

- 5 pounds meaty veal shanks, cut in about 2-inch slices
  Salt, white pepper, and nutmeg
  Flour
- 4 to 6 tablespoons butter or margarine
- ½ pound large mushrooms, quartered
- 1 shallot, finely chopped
- 1 clove garlic, minced or pressed
- ½ teaspoon dried rosemary, crumbled
- 1 cup dry white wine
- ½ cup Rich Chicken Broth (see page 8) or canned chicken broth
- 1 cup whipping cream
  Grated lemon rind, for garnish

1. Sprinkle veal shanks lightly with salt, pepper, and nutmeg. Dust with flour. In a large, deep, heavy frying pan or 4½- to 5-quart Dutch oven over medium heat, melt 4 tablespoons of the butter. Add veal shanks, several at a time, and brown on all sides. Remove shanks as they brown and add more butter as necessary.

2. When all veal shanks are browned, add mushrooms and shallot to pan and brown lightly. Stir in garlic. Return veal shanks to pan and sprinkle with rosemary. Add wine and broth. Bring to a boil, cover, reduce heat, and simmer until veal is very tender (2 to 2½ hours).

3. Blend in cream, increase heat, and boil gently, uncovered, for 15 minutes. Remove veal shanks and mushrooms from liquid to a warm serving dish and keep warm.

4. Bring cooking liquid to a boil over high heat; stir to incorporate brown bits in pan. Cook until slightly thickened and reduced; pour over veal. Sprinkle with grated lemon rind.

Serves 6.

90

CREAMY VEAL STEW WITH SORREL

Sorrel resembles spinach, but its flavor is much more acidic and lemony. Greengrocers who specialize in herbs and unusual lettuces are likely to carry sorrel in the spring and summer. Or you can grow some in your garden as readily as spinach.

1 bunch (3 or 4) leeks
¼ cup butter or margarine
1 bunch (about 6 oz) sorrel, stems removed
3 pounds boneless veal shoulder, cut in 1½-inch cubes
1 teaspoon each salt and Dijon mustard
¼ teaspoon white pepper
1 cup dry white wine
½ cup whipping cream
8 green onions, with about 1½ inches of the leafy tops
8 large mushroom caps

1. Cut off root ends of leeks; remove and discard coarse outer leaves. Cut off and discard green tops so that leeks are about 8 inches long. Split lengthwise, from leafy end, cutting to within about 1 inch of root end. Soak in cold water for several minutes; then separate leaves under running water to rinse away any clinging grit; drain. Slice about ¼ inch thick.

2. In a large, deep frying pan or Dutch oven over medium heat, melt 2 tablespoons of the butter. Add sliced leeks. Cook, stirring often, until limp but not browned. Cut about half of the sorrel leaves into ½-inch slivers; mix into leeks and cook until wilted and bright green. Mix in veal, salt, mustard, pepper, wine, and cream.

3. Bring to a boil, cover, reduce heat, and simmer until veal is very tender (about 1½ hours). Transfer veal to a bowl and keep it warm.

4. Transfer cooking liquid to a blender and purée until smooth. Return purée to cooking pan and bring to a boil over high heat. Cook, uncovered, stirring often, until reduced by about half.

5. In a medium frying pan over moderate heat, melt remaining 2 tablespoons butter. Add green onions and cook until bright green and just tender. (Do not brown.) Remove from pan and keep warm. In same pan, brown mushrooms lightly. Cut remaining sorrel in ¼-inch slivers.

6. To serve, taste sauce and season with salt if needed. Divide veal evenly among 4 warm plates. Pour sauce evenly over veal. Place 2 onions, green stems out, and 2 mushroom caps on each plate. Shower sorrel over veal. Serve at once.

Serves 4.

This veal and sorrel stew was inspired by a blanquette de veau served by Jean-Paul Lacombe at his restaurant, Léon de Lyon. You might add a gratin of potatoes, such as the one on page 102.

**MIDSUMMER
CELEBRATION FOR SIX**

*Sherried Artichoke Soup
(see page 37)*

Pot-Roasted Lemon Veal

New Potatoes

Dilled Carrot Purée

Garlic-Sautéed Zucchini

French Bread

Sweet Butter

Apple Tart Amandine

White Wine

Coffee

*Three vegetables—
new potatoes, a
creamy purée of
carrots, and
zucchini cut into
matchsticks or slices
and sautéed quickly
in garlic butter—
accompany the
tender veal.*

*A white wine such
as a Meursault or
Sancerre is a good
choice with the veal.*

POT-ROASTED LEMON VEAL

2 tablespoons butter or
   margarine
1 tablespoon salad oil
1 boned, rolled, and tied veal
   shoulder roast (3 to 3½ lbs)
1 medium onion, chopped
1 clove garlic, minced or pressed
1 lemon
1 medium carrot, sliced
1 stalk celery, sliced
4 sprigs parsley
1 teaspoon salt
¼ teaspoon white peppercorns
⅛ teaspoon ground nutmeg
1 cup dry white wine
¾ cup whipping cream
   Italian (flat-leaf) parsley, for
   garnish

1. In a 4- to 5-quart Dutch oven or
deep frying pan over medium heat,
melt butter with oil. Add veal and
brown on all sides until golden. As
you turn roast to brown last side, add
onion and garlic around edges, cooking and stirring occasionally until
lightly browned.

2. Meanwhile, grate lemon rind and
reserve it; squeeze juice from lemon.
To browned veal, add lemon juice
and all but 1 teaspoon of the lemon
rind, the carrot, celery, parsley, salt,
peppercorns, nutmeg, and wine.
Bring to a boil, cover, reduce heat,
and simmer until veal is very tender
(1½ to 2 hours).

3. Remove roast to a warm, deep
platter, cover lightly, and keep it
warm. Strain and reserve cooking
liquid, discarding solids. Return liquid
to cooking pan and add cream.

4. Bring to a boil over high heat,
stirring often. Cook and stir until
sauce is slightly reduced and begins
to thicken. Taste, and add salt if
needed. Slice veal and arrange on
platter. Pour sauce over. Garnish with
reserved lemon rind and parsley.

Serves 6.

DILLED CARROT PURÉE

6 medium carrots (about 1 lb),
   thinly sliced
2 cups water
¼ teaspoon each salt and
   dried dill weed
¼ cup whipping cream
2 tablespoons butter or
   margarine
   Pinch each ground nutmeg
   and white pepper

1. In a 2-quart saucepan combine
carrots, the water, salt, and dill weed.
Bring to a boil over high heat; then
cover, reduce heat, and boil gently
until carrots are very tender (20 to 25
minutes).

2. Drain carrots well and transfer to
a food processor or blender. Add
cream and process or whirl until
smooth. Return purée to cooking pan
and place over low heat.

3. Blend in butter, nutmeg, and
pepper. Stir until heated to serving
temperature. Taste, and add salt if
needed.

*Makes about 1⅔ cups, 4 to 6
servings.*

APPLE TART AMANDINE

5 large, tart cooking apples
   (1¾ to 2 lbs)
2 eggs
⅓ cup sugar
¼ cup amaretto liqueur
   Pinch salt
⅔ cup whipping cream
¼ cup sliced almonds
⅓ cup apricot preserves

Press-In Pastry

1½ cups flour
¼ cup sugar
½ cup cold butter
1 egg yolk
½ teaspoon vanilla extract

1. Preheat oven to 450° F. Prepare Press-In Pastry, and press pastry into bottom and up sides of an 11-inch removable-bottom tart pan.

2. Peel apples and cut in halves lengthwise; remove core. Then cut each half in thin lengthwise slices, keeping slices together in apple shape. Arrange in prepared pastry shell, rounded sides up. After placing apple halves in shell, fan out slices slightly to cover most of the pastry.

3. In a medium bowl beat eggs with sugar, amaretto, and salt until well combined. Blend in cream; pour over apples. Sprinkle with almonds.

4. Bake at 450° F for 15 minutes; reduce heat to 350° F. Bake until filling is set and apples are tender (50 minutes to 1 hour). Remove tart from oven and cool on a wire rack.

5. In a small pan over medium heat, stir preserves until melted and bubbling; strain to remove solid pieces and brush glaze evenly over tart.

6. Remove pan sides and serve tart at room temperature.

Makes 1 tart, 6 to 8 servings.

Press-In Pastry In a medium bowl mix flour and sugar. Cut in butter until crumbly. Beat egg yolk with vanilla. With a fork stir egg mixture lightly into flour mixture; then use your hands to press dough together into a smooth, flattened ball.

Tender veal shoulder is cooked in wine with lemon, then sliced, sauced, and garlanded with vegetables. It is accompanied by a carrot purée.

PORK STEWS

All cuts of pork should be well cooked, not only to kill the microscopic parasites that sometimes exist in raw pork, but because the meat is not particularly tasty underdone.

BOHEMIAN PORK GOULASH

Dill seed and caraway seed accent this traditional pork goulash. Noodles are a good foil for the creamy sauce.

- *2 pounds lean boneless pork, cut in ½- by 2-inch strips Salt and white pepper*
- *1 tablespoon each butter or margarine and salad oil*
- *2 medium onions, thinly sliced and separated into rings*
- *1 clove garlic, minced or pressed*
- *1 tablespoon sweet Hungarian paprika*
- *2 teaspoons caraway seed*
- *½ teaspoon dill seed*
- *1 bay leaf*
- *1 cup Sturdy Beef Broth or Rich Chicken Broth (see page 8) or canned broth*
- *⅓ cup dry white wine*
- *1½ teaspoons cornstarch blended with 1 tablespoon water*
- *⅔ cup sour cream Chopped parsley, for garnish*

1. Sprinkle pork strips on all sides with salt and pepper. In a large, heavy frying pan over medium-high heat, melt butter with oil.

2. Add pork strips, about half at a time, and brown well on all sides, removing them as they brown. When all pork is browned, spoon off all but about 2 tablespoons of the pan drippings (if necessary).

3. Add onion and cook, stirring often, until it is soft and begins to brown. Mix in garlic, paprika, caraway seed, and dill seed. Return pork strips (along with any accumulated juices) to pan. Add bay leaf. Pour in broth and wine. Bring to a boil, cover, reduce heat, and simmer until pork is tender (45 to 50 minutes).

4. Remove and discard bay leaf. Blend in the cornstarch mixture and cook, stirring, until sauce boils and thickens. Remove pan from heat and blend in sour cream.

5. Return to low heat and stir gently until heated through. *Do not boil.* Taste, and add salt if needed. Sprinkle with parsley.

Serves 4 to 6.

SPICED PORK CHOPS WITH RHUBARB

At the first rosy blush of spring rhubarb, here is a dish to give a menu a lift. You might accompany the tangy chops with spears of early asparagus to celebrate the season.

- *4 loin pork chops, ½ to ¾ inch thick (1½ to 2 lbs in all)*
- *½ teaspoon ground ginger Salt and white pepper*
- *1 tablespoon each butter or margarine and salad oil*
- *2 cups diced rhubarb*
- *1 shallot, finely chopped (about 2 tbsp)*
- *¼ cup firmly packed brown sugar*
- *¼ teaspoon ground cinnamon*
- *⅛ teaspoon dried rosemary, crumbled*
- *⅔ cup dry white wine Chopped parsley, for garnish*

1. Rub pork chops on all sides with ginger; sprinkle with salt and pepper. In a large, heavy frying pan over medium heat, melt butter with oil. Add chops and brown well on all sides, removing them from pan as they brown.

2. Spoon off all but about 1 generous tablespoon of the pan drippings; then add rhubarb and shallot and cook, stirring gently, until shallot is lightly browned. Stir in brown sugar. Return chops to pan, spooning some of the rhubarb mixture over them.

3. Sprinkle chops with cinnamon and rosemary. Add wine. Bring to a boil, cover, reduce heat, and simmer until tender (40 to 45 minutes).

4. Remove chops to a warm, deep platter and keep warm. Bring rhubarb mixture to a boil over high heat. Cook, stirring, until sauce thickens slightly. Taste, and add salt if needed. Pour over chops. Sprinkle with parsley to garnish, and serve at once.

Serves 4.

PORK CHOPS À LA NORMANDE

Here is a temptingly fruity fall or winter dish—pork chops tenderly simmered with apples, cider, and cream. It's good with rice or fluffy homemade mashed potatoes.

- *4 loin pork chops, ½ to ¾ inch thick (1½ to 2 lbs in all) Salt, white pepper, and nutmeg*
- *2 tablespoons butter or margarine*
- *1 tablespoon salad oil*
- *1 small onion, thinly slivered*
- *2 large, tart cooking apples, peeled, quartered, cored, and thinly sliced*
- *½ cup apple cider or apple juice*
- *1 tablespoon Dijon mustard*
- *½ cup whipping cream Watercress, for garnish*

1. Sprinkle pork chops on all sides with salt, pepper, and nutmeg. In a large, deep, heavy frying pan over medium heat, melt butter with oil. Add chops and brown well on all sides, removing them from the pan as they brown. Pour off and discard all but about 2 tablespoons of the drippings.

2. To same pan add onion and apples and cook, stirring gently, until onions are soft and lightly browned. Return chops to pan, spooning apple and onion mixture over them.

3. In a small bowl blend apple cider with mustard; pour over chops. Add cream. Bring to a boil, cover, reduce heat, and simmer until chops are tender (40 to 45 minutes).

4. Remove chops with most of the apples and onions to a warm, deep platter and keep warm. Bring cooking liquid to a boil over high heat. Cook, stirring, until large, shiny bubbles form and sauce begins to thicken. Taste, and add salt if needed. Pour over chops. Garnish with watercress and serve at once.

Serves 4.

GINGERED PORK STRIPS

Purists will insist that this stew by any other reckoning is a stir-fry. Yet the elements of many stews—meat, onions, mushrooms, celery, carrots, seasonings, and liquid—are here, and the method is a brief version of stew cooking techniques. Whatever it is called, it adds up to a colorful dish of tender pork strips to serve over steamed brown rice.

- 1½ to 2 pounds lean
     boneless pork
- 2 *tablespoons salad oil*
- 1 *medium onion, thinly slivered*
- ½ *pound mushrooms, thinly sliced*
- 1 *clove garlic, minced or pressed*
- 1 *stalk celery, thinly sliced on the diagonal*
- 1 *medium carrot, thinly sliced on the diagonal*
- ¼ *cup each dry sherry and Rich Chicken Broth (see page 8) or canned chicken broth*
- 2 *teaspoons grated fresh ginger or ½ teaspoon ground ginger*
- ¼ *cup soy sauce*
- 2 *tablespoons water*
- 1 *teaspoon sugar*
- 2 *teaspoons cornstarch*
- ¼ *pound edible-pod peas*
- 3 *green onions, thinly sliced on the diagonal*

1. Cut pork in thin strips about ¾ inch wide and 2 inches long. In a large, heavy frying pan or a wok, heat oil over medium-high heat. Add pork strips, about half at a time, and brown on all sides. Remove strips as they brown and set aside.

2. To same pan add onion and mushrooms; cook, stirring, until onion is limp and mushrooms brown lightly. Mix in garlic, celery, and carrot; cook and stir over medium heat for 2 to 3 minutes more. Return browned pork (along with any juices) to pan. Mix in sherry, broth, and ginger. Reduce heat, cover, and simmer for 5 minutes.

3. Meanwhile, in a small bowl blend soy sauce, the water, sugar, and cornstarch. Remove ends and strings from peas and cut each (unless very small) on the diagonal in 3 pieces. Blend soy sauce mixture into pork and vegetables. Stir in peas and green onions. Cook, uncovered, stirring constantly, over medium-high heat until sauce boils and thickens and peas are just tender and bright green. Serve at once.

Serves 4 to 6.

Stew in a wok? Why not? It's a perfect pan for cooking Gingered Pork Strips. However, you can prepare this colorful dish in a large, heavy frying pan, if you prefer.

SMOKED PORK WITH MUSTARD-GLAZED ONIONS

In the Alsace region of eastern France, this traditional dish is called *schiffala*. Add an innovative side dish: tiny onions cooked in some of the broth and finished with mustard and cream.

- 1 leek
- 1 smoked pork shoulder (5 to 7 lbs); also called a picnic
- 1 carrot, thinly sliced
- 1 medium onion, thinly slivered
- 1 celery root (½ to ¾ lb), peeled and julienned (2-in. strips)
  Half a bay leaf
- 2 cups Alsatian Sylvaner or other dry white wine
- 8 cups water
- 24 small white boiling onions (about 1¼ lbs)
- 1 tablespoon Dijon mustard
- ¼ cup whipping cream
  Chopped parsley, for garnish

1. Remove root end and top of leek; soak briefly, rinse carefully, and slice about ½ inch thick.

2. Place meat in a deep 6- to 8-quart kettle. Add leek, carrot, onion, celery root, and bay leaf. Pour in wine and the water. Bring to a boil over medium heat, cover, reduce heat, and simmer until meat is very tender when pierced (3 to 3½ hours).

3. About 30 minutes before meat is done, place onions in a 2-quart saucepan. Ladle out 2 cups of the broth in the kettle and pour over onions. Bring to a boil, reduce heat, and boil gently, uncovered, until onions are tender when pierced with a fork (12 to 15 minutes). Pour off all but about ¼ cup of the cooking liquid. Blend in mustard and cream. Increase heat to medium and cook, stirring, until large, shiny bubbles form and sauce thickens slightly.

4. Remove meat to a board, remove and discard rind, and slice to serve with onions. Sprinkle parsley over sliced meat and onions.

Serves 10 to 12.

BAVARIAN MARINATED PORK

Here, a pork loin roast gets the sauerbraten treatment—marinating in vinegar and wine with spices.

- 3 cups (750-ml bottle) off-dry or dry white wine
- 2 medium onions, thinly sliced and separated into rings
- 1 carrot, thinly sliced
- 2 bay leaves
- 1 teaspoon each *whole cloves and slivered crystallized ginger*
- 1 tablespoon pickling spices
- ½ teaspoon each *black peppercorns and dried thyme*
- 1 clove garlic, slivered
- ½ cup apple cider vinegar
- 1 pork loin (3½ to 4 lbs)
- 2 tablespoons butter
- 1 tablespoon each *sugar and tomato paste*
- 2 teaspoons salt
- ¼ cup golden raisins
- 2 tablespoons cornstarch, blended with 2 tablespoons water

1. In a 2½- to 3-quart saucepan, heat wine, onions, carrot, bay leaves, cloves, ginger, pickling spices, peppercorns, thyme, and garlic. Remove from heat; stir in vinegar. Pour over roast in a large, deep bowl. Cover and refrigerate for 24 to 48 hours, turning meat occasionally.

2. Pat roast dry; reserve marinade. In a 5½- to 6-quart Dutch oven over medium heat, melt butter and brown roast on all sides. Spoon off fat; add marinade. Blend in sugar, tomato paste, and salt. Bring to a boil, cover, reduce heat, and simmer until meat is very tender (2½ to 3 hours).

3. Remove meat and keep it warm. Strain and degrease cooking liquid. Return to Dutch oven over high heat. Add raisins. Boil until reduced by about a third.

4. Remove from heat and blend in cornstarch mixture. Boil, stirring constantly, until thickened and clear. Taste, and add salt if needed. Slice pork and serve with sauce.

Serves 6 to 8.

CONNIE'S PORK AND CHICKEN ADOBO

Pork combines with chicken in equal proportions to make a favorite Filipino dish. Accompany it with rice. Although it is not traditional to serve an adobo with plain vegetables, steamed asparagus or tender-crisp edible-pod peas taste good with it.

- 1½ pounds chicken breasts
- 1½ pounds chicken thighs
- 2 tablespoons salad oil
- 3 pounds lean, boneless pork, cut in 1-inch cubes
- 6 cloves garlic, minced or pressed
- ½ cup each *soy sauce and water*
- ⅓ cup distilled white vinegar
  Chopped parsley or thinly sliced green onions, for garnish

1. Remove skin and bones from chicken breasts; remove skin from thighs (bone as well, if you wish, or use a cleaver to chop thighs in half).

2. In a large frying pan, heat oil over medium heat. Add chicken pieces and pork, about half of each at a time (do not crowd pan), and brown lightly on all sides. Remove and reserve chicken and pork as they brown. When all the meat is browned and removed from pan, discard fat.

3. Return meats to pan. Mix in garlic, soy sauce, the water, and vinegar. Bring to a boil, cover, reduce heat, and simmer until meats are very tender (40 to 45 minutes).

4. Using a slotted spoon, transfer meats to a warm serving bowl and keep warm. Increase heat to high and boil cooking liquid, stirring occasionally, until reduced by about a third. Pour over meat. Sprinkle with parsley before serving.

Serves 8 to 10.

LAMB STEWS

When lamb's not in season in this country, frozen New Zealand lamb can be found in most stores. Therefore it is almost always available the year around and no longer referred to as spring lamb. From three to five months old, it is called baby lamb; from five months to one year, just lamb; and older than a year, mutton. Mutton is stronger flavored and tougher than lamb and should be cooked longer.

When people claim to dislike lamb because of its strong flavor, it is generally because they have been served this delicate meat by a cook who failed to remove the papery membrane that covers most cuts. When cooked, this membrane is responsible for the strong flavor. It should therefore be removed before the meat is cooked.

Good-quality lamb can be recognized by the firmness of the flesh and the whiteness of the fat. The cuts most often used for stews are boneless leg, shoulder, neck, and breast.

Because many people do not enjoy the flavor of lamb fat and because it congeals so quickly, it is advisable to remove all the surface fat before serving a lamb stew.

LAMB STEW WITH ARTICHOKES

Assertively spiced and cooked with red pepper and currants, this generous lamb stew has a sweet-sour flavor suggestive of Sicilian cuisine. Serve it with steamed rice or a pilaf, and green beans.

> 4 pounds bone-in lamb neck
>   or shoulder, in large pieces
>   Salt and pepper
> 3 tablespoons olive oil
> 1 large onion, slivered
> 1 medium carrot, shredded
> 1 stalk celery, thinly sliced
> 1 red or green bell pepper,
>   seeded and chopped
> 3 cloves garlic, minced or
>   pressed

> ¼ cup dried currants
> ½ teaspoon each ground
>   cinnamon and dried oregano
> ¼ teaspoon ground allspice
> 1 large can (28 oz) tomatoes
> 1 can (6 oz) tomato paste
> 1 cup Rich Chicken Broth
>   (see page 8) or canned
>   chicken broth
> 1 package (9 oz) frozen
>   artichoke hearts
> 2 tablespoons lemon juice
>   Grated lemon rind and
>   chopped parsley, for garnish

1. Sprinkle lamb lightly with salt and pepper. In a 5- to 6-quart Dutch oven, heat oil over medium heat. Add lamb, about half at a time, and brown on all sides. Remove pieces as they brown, and reserve them.

2. Spoon off all except about 2 tablespoons of the drippings. Add onion, carrot, celery, and bell pepper. Cook, stirring often, until onion is soft and begins to brown. Mix in garlic. Return the browned meat to pan. Add currants. Sprinkle with cinnamon, oregano, and allspice. Add tomatoes (coarsely chopped) and their liquid, tomato paste, and broth. Bring to a boil, cover, reduce heat, and simmer until lamb is very tender (about 2 hours).

3. Skim and discard as much surface fat as possible; then simmer, uncovered, until sauce is thick (20 to 30 minutes). Meanwhile, cook artichokes according to package directions. Drain well and mix lightly into stew. Blend in lemon juice. Taste, and add salt if needed.

4. Serve sprinkled with lemon rind and parsley.

Serves 8.

SPRING LAMB STEW WITH FRESH PEAS

Fresh mint seasons the lamb in this glistening stew. Shell fresh peas to be sure it will taste like spring!

> 3 pounds boneless lamb leg
>   or shoulder, fat trimmed,
>   cut in 1-inch cubes
>   Salt and white pepper
> 3 tablespoons butter or
>   margarine
> 2 teaspoons salad oil
> 3 shallots, finely chopped
> 1 clove garlic, minced or pressed
> 1 large carrot, sliced about
>   ¼ inch thick
> 3 or 4 sprigs fresh mint
> 1 cup Rich Chicken Broth
>   (see page 8) or canned
>   chicken broth
> 1½ cups dry white wine
> 1½ to 2 cups shelled fresh peas

1. Sprinkle lamb lightly with salt and pepper. In a large, deep frying pan or Dutch oven, melt 2 tablespoons of the butter with the oil. Add lamb, about a third at a time. Brown well, removing lamb as it browns. When all lamb is removed from pan, add shallots, cooking and stirring until they are soft and lightly browned. Mix in garlic and carrot.

2. Return lamb to pan. Add mint, broth, and wine. Bring to a boil, cover, reduce heat, and simmer until tender (45 minutes to 1 hour).

3. Remove lamb and keep it warm. Strain cooking liquid, discarding carrot and mint. Skim and discard surface fat. Return liquid to pan and bring to a boil over high heat. Cook, stirring, until slightly reduced and syrupy. Taste, and add salt if needed. Mix in peas and cook, stirring, for 1 to 2 minutes.

4. Cut remaining 1 tablespoon butter in pieces. Off heat, stir in butter, one piece at a time, until melted.

5. Return lamb to sauce, stirring to coat well. Spoon lamb into center of each warm plate. Surround with sauce and peas and serve at once.

Serves 6 to 8.

This savory lamb stew is baked in a deep casserole that can be brought directly to the table. Serve it with toast on which to spread the roasted garlic.

BAKED LAMB STEW WITH GARLIC TOAST

Here is an easily assembled lamb stew of French origin—as you might guess from the pungent accompaniment of toast spread with roasted garlic. Serve each diner several cloves to squeeze out onto the toast.

> 3 pounds boneless lamb,
> well trimmed of fat,
> cut in large cubes
> 2 cloves garlic, minced
> or pressed
> 1 teaspoon salt
> ½ teaspoon dried thyme
> ⅛ teaspoon pepper
> 2 medium carrots, sliced
> ½ inch thick
> 2 medium onions, thinly sliced
> and separated into rings
> ½ cup pitted ripe olives
> 1 bay leaf
> 2 strips orange rind, each
> about ½ inch by 3 inches
> 3 tablespoons butter
> or margarine
> ½ cup ham strips, ½ inch thick
> by 1½ inches long
> ¼ cup brandy
> 1 can (1 lb) tomatoes
> 1 tablespoon flour
> Snipped fresh chives or finely
> chopped parsley, for garnish
> Toasted French bread

Roasted Garlic

> 1 whole bulb garlic (unpeeled)

1. Preheat oven to 350° F. Sprinkle lamb cubes with mixture of garlic, salt, thyme, and pepper. Place half of the lamb in a deep 4- to 5-quart casserole. Add, in layers, carrots; onions; and olives, bay leaf, and orange rind.

2. In a small frying pan over medium heat, melt 2 tablespoons of the butter. Add ham strips and cook until lightly browned. Stir in brandy, scraping up pan drippings. Spoon ham mixture over vegetables in casserole. Drain tomatoes, reserving liquid; chop tomatoes coarsely and add to casserole. Cover with remaining lamb cubes. Pour in reserved tomato liquid.

3. Cover and bake for 1½ hours; stir lightly; then cover again and bake until lamb is nearly tender (about 1 hour). While lamb cooks, prepare Roasted Garlic.

4. Meanwhile, in a small bowl soften remaining 1 tablespoon butter and blend smoothly with flour; set aside.

5. Skim and discard all surface fat. Stir butter mixture into the liquid; bake, uncovered, until the lamb is tender and the sauce is thickened (about 20 minutes).

6. Serve sprinkled with chives and accompanied by pieces of toasted French bread on which to spread the cloves of roasted garlic.

Serves 6 to 8.

Roasted Garlic Place garlic in a small baking pan and bake with stew during last hour of cooking, until center cloves feel soft and buttery. Let cool slightly before serving; then separate quickly into individual cloves.

OVEN-BAKED IRON-POT LAMB STEW

This lamb stew is particularly easy to prepare and cook—the meat is simply layered in a cast-iron pot with a variety of vegetables and then baked. Once it is in the oven, you can get on with other chores. This stew comes from the sheep-raising country of California's Mendocino County.

> 2 pounds lean, boneless lamb
> shoulder, cut in 1-inch cubes
> 1½ teaspoons salt
> ½ teaspoon each ground
> allspice and dried
> rosemary, crumbled
> ¼ teaspoon pepper
> 1 clove garlic, minced or pressed
> 1 large onion, quartered,
> then thinly sliced
> 4 medium carrots, sliced
> about ½ inch thick
> 2 cups coarsely sliced cabbage
> 3 medium-sized new potatoes,
> scrubbed and sliced (un-
> peeled) about ¼ inch thick
> 1 can (8 oz) tomato sauce
> 1 cup dry white wine

1. Preheat oven to 375° F. In a large bowl lightly mix cubed lamb with a mixture of salt, allspice, rosemary, pepper, and garlic.

2. In a deep 3½- to 4-quart cast-iron casserole or Dutch oven, place, in layers, half each of the seasoned lamb, onion, carrot, cabbage, and potato. Repeat layers, ending with potatoes. Pour tomato sauce and wine over the mixture.

3. Cover and bake until both the lamb and vegetables are tender, potatoes are lightly browned, and most of the liquid has been absorbed (about 2½ to 3 hours).

Serves 6.

LAMB CHOPS IN BEER

Lamb shoulder chops are simmered to tenderness in beer with a variety of vegetables to make this succulent meal-in-one-dish.

The preparation is simple and the cooking time is less than an hour, making this recipe an ideal candidate for an evening when you're late home from the office.

    4   lamb shoulder chops, ½ to ¾ inch thick (about 2 lbs in all)
        Salt, pepper, and ground cloves
    3   tablespoons butter or margarine
    1   large onion, slivered
    3   medium carrots, thinly sliced
    1   large clove garlic, minced or pressed
    2   medium tomatoes, chopped
    ¼   cup chopped parsley
    ¼   teaspoon dried thyme
    3   medium potatoes (1 to 1¼ lbs), each cut lengthwise in 8 wedges
    1   bottle or can (12 oz) beer
    1   tablespoon flour

1. Lightly sprinkle lamb chops on all sides with salt, pepper, and cloves. Reserve 1 tablespoon of the butter in a small bowl. In a large, heavy frying pan over medium-high heat, melt remaining butter. Add lamb chops and brown well on all sides, removing them as they brown. Spoon off all but about 2 tablespoons of the drippings (if necessary).

2. To same pan add onion; cook, stirring often, until lightly browned. Mix in carrots, garlic, tomatoes, 3 tablespoons of the parsley, and the thyme. Add potatoes.

3. Arrange lamb chops over potatoes. Pour in beer. Bring to a boil, cover, reduce heat, and simmer until lamb chops are tender (40 to 45 minutes). Meanwhile, blend flour smoothly with reserved butter.

4. Remove lamb chops to a warm, deep serving platter. With a slotted spoon remove carrots and potatoes and spoon them over and around chops. Skim and discard surface fat from cooking liquid. Bring liquid to a boil over high heat, stirring often; cook until reduced by about a fourth. Blend in flour mixture, bit by bit, stirring until sauce thickens and boils. Taste, and add salt if needed. Pour over lamb and vegetables.

5. Sprinkle with the reserved 1 table-spoon parsley before serving.

Serves 4.

LAMB MEATBALL IRISH STEW

All the colorful elements you expect in an Irish stew are included and combined in this appetizing and time-saving dish. At the heart of it are ground-lamb meatballs. Potatoes are not cooked in the stew, but small whole ones—boiled or steamed and buttered—would be good to offer as a side dish.

In acknowledgment of the country of origin, it would be appropriate to bake a loaf of homemade Irish soda bread to accompany this stew.

    2   tablespoons butter or margarine
    1   tablespoon salad oil
    ½   pound mushrooms, sliced
    1   large onion, finely chopped
    1   clove garlic, minced or pressed
    ¼   teaspoon each *dried marjoram and savory*
    ⅛   teaspoon ground allspice
    3   medium carrots, sliced about ¼ inch thick
    2   small turnips, peeled, quartered lengthwise, and sliced about ¼ inch thick
    1   cup Sturdy Beef Broth (see page 8) or canned regular-strength beef broth
    2   teaspoons flour
    ¼   cup shelled fresh or frozen peas
        Salt (optional)

Lamb Meatballs

    1   egg
    1   teaspoon salt
        Pinch pepper
    1   tablespoon chopped parsley
    ¼   cup soft bread crumbs
    1½ pounds ground lamb

1. Place 1 tablespoon of the butter in a small bowl and set aside to soften.

2. Prepare Lamb Meatballs. In a large, deep, heavy frying pan over medium-high heat, melt remaining butter with oil. Add meatballs, about half at a time, and brown on all sides, turning carefully. Remove meatballs from pan as they brown.

3. When all meatballs are browned, pour off all but about 2 tablespoons of the pan drippings (if necessary). Add mushrooms and cook, stirring often, until lightly browned. Add onion and cook until soft. Mix in garlic, marjoram, savory, and allspice.

4. Return meatballs to pan. Add carrots, turnips, and broth. Bring to a boil, cover, reduce heat, and simmer until vegetables are tender (25 to 30 minutes). Meanwhile, mix flour smoothly with the softened butter.

5. Using a slotted spoon, remove meatballs and vegetables to a warm serving dish and keep them warm. If necessary, skim and discard fat from cooking liquid; then stir liquid to blend in brown bits from pan. Bring to a boil over medium-high heat. Add flour mixture, a bit at a time, stirring until sauce thickens and boils. Mix in peas and cook just until heated through. Taste, and add salt if needed. Pour sauce over meatball mixture and serve at once.

Serves 4 to 6.

Lamb Meatballs In a medium bowl beat egg. Mix in salt, pepper, parsley, and bread crumbs. Lightly mix in ground lamb. Shape in 1-inch balls.

Containing turnips, carrots, mushrooms, and peas, Lamb Meatball Irish Stew has all the flavor of the more time-consuming traditional version.

FIRESIDE SUPPER

Sausage in Wine Savoyard

Potato Gratin

*Green Salad With
Toasted Walnuts*

Country French Bread

Butter

*Wine-Poached Pears With
Raspberry Sauce*

Milk

White Wine

Coffee

---

*From the firesides of
the French alpine
region of the Savoy
comes this winter
sausage supper.*

*To complement the
sausage, bake a
crisp gratin of
potatoes—quick to
assemble if you use
your food processor
to shred the cheese
and slice the
potatoes. Winter
pears sauced with a
crimson purée of
frozen raspberries
complete this repast.*

SAUSAGE IN WINE SAVOYARD

 1¼ to 1½ pounds Polish sausage
   or garlic sausage
  2 tablespoons butter or
   margarine
  2 medium onions, thinly
   slivered
  ½ teaspoon dried rosemary,
   crumbled
  3 medium tomatoes, seeded
   and chopped
  1 teaspoon Dijon mustard
  ½ cup dry white wine
   Salt
   Chopped parsley, for garnish

1. With a fork, pierce sausage in several places on all sides. In a large, deep, heavy frying pan over medium heat, melt butter. Add sausage and brown lightly on one side.

2. Turn sausage, add onions and rosemary, and continue cooking, stirring often, until onions brown lightly. Add tomatoes, mustard, and wine. Bring to a very gentle boil; then cover, reduce heat, and simmer for about 20 minutes.

3. Remove sausage to a warm platter and keep it warm. Bring tomato mixture to a boil over high heat and cook, stirring, until it thickens slightly. Taste, and add salt if needed. Spoon over sausage and garnish with a sprinkling of parsley.

4. Cut ring of sausage in generous chunks to serve.

Serves 4.

POTATO GRATIN

  4 medium baking potatoes
   (1¾ to 2 lbs)
  1 clove garlic, split
  3 tablespoons butter or
   margarine
   Salt, white pepper, and
   ground nutmeg
  ½ pound Gruyère or Swiss cheese,
   shredded (2 cups)
  ½ cup Sturdy Beef Broth
   (see page 8) or canned
   regular-strength beef broth

1. Preheat oven to 400° F. Slice potatoes very thinly. (Use food processor with thin slicing blade if possible.) Rub a shallow oval or rectangular 2-quart baking dish with cut sides of the split clove of garlic. Then butter dish generously, using about a fourth of the butter.

2. Spread about a third of the potatoes in baking dish; sprinkle lightly with salt, pepper, and nutmeg. Scatter about a third of the cheese over potatoes. Repeat layers with remaining potatoes, seasonings, and cheese, ending with a layer of cheese. Dot top with remaining butter.

3. Bring broth to a boil; then pour slowly over potatoes.

4. Bake, uncovered, until potatoes are tender and top is crusty and well browned (45 minutes to 1 hour). Serve very hot.

Serves 4.

WINE-POACHED PEARS WITH RASPBERRY SAUCE

 1½ cups dry red wine
  ¾ cup sugar
   Half a lemon, thinly sliced
  4 firm-ripe medium to large
   pears, peeled and cored
   from bottom
  1 teaspoon vanilla extract

Raspberry Sauce

   Half a 12-ounce package
   unsweetened frozen raspberries, thawed slightly
  2 tablespoons kirsch
  ⅓ cup confectioners' sugar

1. In a deep saucepan large enough to hold all the pears side by side, combine wine, sugar, and lemon slices. Bring mixture to a boil, stirring until sugar dissolves.

2. Add pears to boiling wine mixture. Cover, reduce heat, and simmer, turning pears occasionally to cover with liquid, until they are tender when pierced with a fork (15 to 20 minutes). Remove from heat, remove and discard lemon slices, blend in vanilla, and let pears cool in wine mixture at room temperature.

3. Prepare Raspberry Sauce.

4. Serve pears standing upright in shallow dishes, at room temperature or chilled. Spoon Raspberry Sauce over each serving.

Serves 4.

Raspberry Sauce In blender or food processor purée raspberries, kirsch, and sugar. Strain through a fine sieve to remove seeds.

Makes about ¾ cup.

Garlic sausage—either a large ring or links— served with crisp Potato Gratin, bread, and a green salad is a meal that can be prepared quickly after a day of skiing, and enjoyed while sitting around a blazing fire.

Not only is chicken a dependable money saver, it also cooks quickly. Honeyed Chicken With Apricots (see page 114) can be prepared in about an hour.

Succulent Poultry & Fish Stews

There was a time when the chicken that went into the stewpot was a stewing hen—an ample bird of a certain age. These days, unless you shop at a special poultry store it's hard to find such flavorful chickens. But you can still achieve rich-tasting stews with a young frying chicken weighing 3 pounds or more. The harvest from the sea reaps an astonishing variety of fish and shellfish, and many markets offer a good selection of whole and filleted fish to use in the recipes that follow.

POULTRY STEWS

The versatile chicken is a stewpot favorite. When it is cooked to juicy tenderness in broth, wine, or cream, chicken is a dish that just about everyone likes. And if you have an eye to economical entertaining, look to one of the chicken stews that follow for a dazzling dinner party dish that won't break the budget.

Although the traditional stewing hen is hard to find nowadays, a frying chicken is an acceptable alternative. The chicken recipes that follow were all tested with such birds, with seasonings filling in for any flavor failings one might attribute to their youth.

BAKED CHICKEN IN RED WINE

When the French serve chicken in wine, or coq au vin, they usually accompany it with boiled potatoes. But why not serve it with baked potatoes? They can go into the oven with the stew for the last 45 minutes to an hour.

> 3 to 3½ pounds meaty chicken pieces (thighs, drumsticks, and breasts)
> ½ teaspoon dried thyme
> ¼ teaspoon each dried rosemary and marjoram
> 1 teaspoon salt
> ⅛ teaspoon pepper
> 2 cloves garlic, minced or pressed
> 1 medium onion, thinly slivered
> 1 medium carrot, shredded
> ½ cup julienned ham strips
> 1 bay leaf
> 1½ cups dry red wine
> 3 tablespoons butter or margarine
> ¾ pound large mushrooms, quartered
> 10 small white boiling onions
> ¼ cup brandy
> 2 tablespoons flour
> Chopped parsley, for garnish

1. Place chicken pieces in a large bowl. Add thyme, rosemary, marjoram, salt, pepper, garlic, onion, carrot, and ham; mix gently. Insert bay leaf in center. Pour wine over chicken mixture. Cover and refrigerate, mixing lightly once or twice, for 8 to 24 hours.

2. Preheat oven to 375° F. Remove chicken from marinade and pat dry, reserving marinade. In a large frying pan, melt 2 tablespoons of the butter; add chicken pieces, about half at a time, and brown well on all sides. As they brown, transfer to a 3½- to 4-quart casserole. Then, to same pan add mushrooms and boiling onions; cook, stirring often, until lightly browned. Add to chicken mixture. Stir a little of the wine from marinade into pan to dissolve drippings; add to chicken. Then mix in remaining marinade.

3. In a small, long-handled pan over low heat, warm brandy gently until it is barely warm to the touch. Ignite and pour, flaming, over chicken.

4. Cover casserole and bake, stirring lightly once or twice, for 1¼ hours. Meanwhile, in a small bowl soften remaining 1 tablespoon butter and blend smoothly with flour; set aside.

5. Remove casserole from oven. Skim and discard surface fat. Add butter mixture, in bits, to casserole, stirring carefully. Cover again and return to oven. Bake until chicken is tender and sauce is thickened (about 30 minutes).

6. Sprinkle with parsley to serve.

Serves 6 to 8.

CHICKEN IN CIDER AND CREAM

This chicken entrée, known as *poulet Vallée d'Auge*, originates in Normandy, an apple-growing region. Hence the use of cider and Calvados.

> 1 chicken (3½ to 4 lbs), cut in quarters
> Salt, white pepper, and nutmeg
> 2 tablespoons butter or margarine
> 1 tablespoon salad oil
> 2 shallots, thinly slivered (about ¼ cup)
> ¾ pound large mushrooms, quartered
> ½ cup Calvados (French apple brandy) or applejack
> 1 cup hard cider
> 1 cup whipping cream
> Apple slices sautéed in butter, for garnish

1. Sprinkle chicken quarters on all sides with salt, pepper, and nutmeg. In a large, deep, heavy frying pan or Dutch oven over medium heat, melt buter with oil. Add chicken pieces and brown well on all sides, removing pieces as they brown. To same pan add shallots and mushrooms and cook, stirring often, until lightly browned. Return chicken to pan.

2. In a small, long-handled pan over low heat, warm Calvados gently until it is barely warm to the touch. Ignite it and pour, flaming, over chicken; stir carefully with a long-handled spoon until flames go out. Add cider. Bring to a boil, cover, reduce heat, and simmer until chicken is very tender (about 1 hour).

3. Transfer chicken pieces to a warm, deep serving platter. Skim and discard fat from cooking liquid.

4. Stir cream into cooking liquid and bring mixture to a boil over high heat, stirring often. Boil until large, shiny bubbles form and liquid is reduced and slightly thickened. Taste; add salt if needed. Pour over chicken.

5. Garnish with sautéed apple slices and serve.

Serves 4.

SPICED ORANGE CHICKEN

Marinating the chicken first in orange liqueur and fresh orange juice and rind ensures flavor that is as deep as it is delicious. To emphasize the citrus taste and to decorate the finished dish, sprinkle the top with thinly slivered orange rind.

> 1 chicken (3 to 3½ lbs), cut in quarters
>
> ½ teaspoon each *salt and dried tarragon*
>
> ¼ teaspoon each *ground nutmeg, whole cloves, and whole allspice*
>
> 1 *clove garlic, minced or pressed*
>
> 1 *tablespoon grated orange rind*
>
> 1 *tablespoon grated fresh ginger or ½ teaspoon ground ginger*
>
> 1 *cup orange juice*
>
> ½ *cup dry white wine*
>
> ¼ *cup orange-flavored liqueur*
>
> 2 *tablespoons butter or margarine*
>
> 1 *tablespoon salad oil*
>
> 3 *shallots, thinly slivered (about ⅓ cup)*
>
> ½ *cup whipping cream*
>
> 1 *tablespoon lemon juice Seedless grapes and thinly slivered orange rind, for garnish*

1. Place chicken quarters in a large, deep bowl. Add salt, tarragon, nutmeg, cloves, allspice, garlic, grated orange rind, ginger, orange juice, wine, and liqueur. Mix lightly and turn the chicken pieces in the marinade; then cover and refrigerate for at least 8 hours and up to 24 hours.

2. Remove chicken from marinade and pat dry. Strain marinade, discarding seasonings. In a large, deep, heavy frying pan or Dutch oven over medium heat, melt butter with oil. Add chicken and brown lightly on all sides; as you turn chicken pieces to brown them on last sides, add shallots to pan around chicken.

3. When chicken is browned, pour in marinade. Bring to a boil, cover, reduce heat, and simmer until chicken is tender (about 1 hour). Remove chicken pieces to a warm serving dish and keep warm.

4. Skim and discard surface fat from cooking liquid. Add cream to liquid and bring mixture to a boil over high heat, stirring frequently. Boil until large, shiny bubbles form and liquid is reduced and slightly thickened. Stir in lemon juice. Taste, and add salt if needed. Pour over chicken.

5. Garnish with grapes and slivered orange rind.

Serves 4.

Serve Spiced Orange Chicken with rice and peas or green beans. A fruity white wine, such as a Chenin Blanc or a spicy Gewürztraminer, is a good complement to this meal.

TRUFFLED-CHICKEN DINNER

Smoked Salmon Terrine

Hot Toast

Chicken in Half-Mourning

Fresh Peas Cooked With New Potatoes

Pear Tarte Tatin

White Wine

Coffee

For every dedicated cook there comes a time for a splurge, and this is a menu for such an occasion. It begins with saumon en rillettes, a buttery terrine of fresh salmon striped with smoked salmon, and continues with a French classic— poulet en demi-deuil, or Chicken in Half-Mourning—that gets its name from the black truffles slipped under the skin. The extravaganza concludes with an elegant upside-down fruit tart.

SMOKED SALMON TERRINE

    1 salmon fillet (¾ lb)
    ½ cup unsalted butter, softened
    2 tablespoons lemon juice
    ⅛ teaspoon cayenne pepper
    ¼ to ½ pound sliced smoked
       salmon, cut in ½-inch-
       wide strips
       Butter lettuce leaves
       Lemon and tomato wedges,
       for garnish

1. Place salmon fillet on a rack over about ½ inch of water in a medium frying pan. Bring water to a boil, cover, reduce heat, and steam salmon until it flakes when tested with a fork (6 to 8 minutes). Remove and discard skin and any bones. Let salmon cool.

2. In food processor combine steamed salmon fillet, butter, lemon juice, and cayenne. Process until smooth. Mix in smoked salmon strips.

3. Spread in a buttered small loaf pan (about 3½ inches by 7 inches). Cover and refrigerate until firm (several hours or overnight).

4. Turn out terrine and slice it about ½ inch thick. Serve on lettuce leaves, garnished with lemon and tomato wedges. Serve with hot toast.

Serves 10 to 12 as a first course.

CHICKEN IN HALF-MOURNING

    1 can (25 g) black truffles or
       1 fresh black truffle, about
       1¼ inches in diameter
    2 tablespoons Madeira (if
       using a fresh truffle)
    2 whole chickens (3 to
       3½ lbs each)
    1 medium onion, sliced and
       separated into rings
    1 medium carrot, sliced
    1 stalk celery, sliced
    ¼ teaspoon white peppercorns
    3 sprigs parsley
    4 cups Rich Chicken Broth
       (see page 8) or 2 cans
       (14½ oz each) chicken broth
       and ½ cup water
    3 tablespoons butter or
       margarine

    ¼ cup flour
    ½ cup whipping cream
    2 tablespoons lemon juice
       Salt

1. Drain and reserve liquid from canned truffles. Cut 12 thin slices from a truffle; finely chop rest of truffle(s). Place in bowl with liquid (or Madeira, if using a fresh truffle).

2. Rinse chickens and pat dry; reserve giblets for another use. Remove and discard any excess fat. With two fingers, reach into each chicken from neck end and carefully loosen skin from flesh across breasts and tops of drumsticks. Using 6 truffle slices for each chicken, gently slide truffles under skin across breast and tops of drumsticks. Fasten neck and body cavities of each chicken with a skewer. Place chickens side by side in a deep, heavy Dutch oven just large enough to hold them both.

3. To chickens add onion, carrot, celery, peppercorns, parsley, and broth. Bring broth to a boil over medium heat; then cover, reduce heat, and simmer until chickens are very tender when thighs are pierced with a fork (about 1½ hours). Remove chickens to a warm platter; cover with foil and keep warm.

4. Strain cooking liquid, discarding vegetables. Skim and discard fat. Return liquid to a boil over high heat, uncovered, until reduced to 2½ cups. Remove from heat.

5. In a 2- to 3-quart saucepan over medium heat, melt butter. Blend in flour; cook and stir until bubbly. Remove from heat; gradually blend in the 2½ cups reduced chicken broth. Cook, stirring, until thickened and boiling. Blend in cream and return to a boil, stirring often. Stir in lemon juice and chopped truffles plus liquid (or Madeira). Add salt if needed.

6. Spoon about a third of the sauce over and around chickens on serving platter; serve remainder in a warm sauceboat. Use poultry shears to cut chickens into quarters to serve.

Serves 8.

PEAR TARTE TATIN

   1 tablespoon butter or
     margarine
1¼ cups sugar
   3 tablespoons flour
   1 teaspoon ground cinnamon
     Pinch salt
   1 tablespoon lemon juice
   4 large pears, peeled, halved,
     cored, thinly sliced, and
     tossed with lemon juice
     (about 8 cups slices)

Flaky Pastry

   1 cup flour
     Pinch salt
   ¼ cup cold butter
   1 tablespoon lard
1½ to 2½ tablespoons cold water

1. Prepare Flaky Pastry. Spread butter over bottom and sides of a 9-inch round cake pan. In a heavy frying pan, heat 1 cup of the sugar over moderately high heat, tipping and tilting pan so that sugar melts evenly, until it is completely melted and a rich amber color. Pour the caramel syrup into the buttered pan to coat the bottom evenly. Place pan on a rack until caramel hardens.

2. Preheat oven to 450° F. In a small bowl blend the remaining ¼ cup sugar with the flour, cinnamon, and salt. In a large bowl mix lemon juice with sliced pears; add flour mixture, mixing lightly to coat slices. Arrange pear slices in caramel-lined pan.

3. Roll out pastry and place it over pears; trim edge so that it extends over pan edge by about 1 inch. Fold edge of pastry under, pressing it against inside edge of pan. Slash top of pastry in several places to permit steam to escape.

4. Bake on lowest rack of oven until pastry is well browned and pears are tender when tested with a fork (40 to 45 minutes).

5. To serve shortly after baking, let tart stand in pan just until juices stop bubbling. Then invert hot tart carefully onto a warm serving plate. Let stand with baking pan in place for about 5 minutes; then remove pan

and serve hot. If any caramel remains on pan bottom, place pan over direct medium heat until caramel softens; then use a spatula to spread it over pears. If tart is made ahead, leave it in baking pan on a wire rack for as long as 4 hours, until about 20 minutes before serving. Reheat, uncovered, in baking pan in a 350°F oven for 20 minutes. Then invert onto serving plate and proceed as if the tart had just been baked.

Makes 1 pie, 8 servings.

Flaky Pastry In a medium bowl mix flour and salt. With a pastry blender cut in butter and lard until mixture resembles coarse crumbs. Mixing lightly with a fork, gradually blend in the cold water, stirring just until mixture begins to cling together. Use your hands to form pastry into a flattened ball. Roll out on a floured board or pastry cloth to a 13-inch-diameter round.

This menu, intended for a very special occasion, features chicken bathed in a creamy truffled sauce. The entire production takes only one truffle (canned or fresh). A California Chardonnay or Fumé Blanc is a good wine choice with this chicken.

BRAISED CHICKEN IN CREAM WITH ASPARAGUS

Emerald spears of fresh spring asparagus share the subtly flavored cream sauce of this elegant chicken dish.

- *3 to 3½ pounds meaty chicken pieces (thighs, drumsticks, and breasts)*
  Salt and white pepepr
- *2 tablespoons butter or margarine*
- *½ teaspoon dried savory*
  Pinch ground cloves
- *1 teaspoon grated lemon rind*
- *6 green onions, cut in 1-inch pieces (use about 3 inches of top of each)*
- *½ cup each dry vermouth and Rich Chicken Broth (see page 8) or canned chicken broth*
- *1 cup whipping cream*
- *1 to 1½ pounds asparagus spears*
- *1 egg yolk*
- *2 tablespoons lemon juice*

1. Sprinkle chicken with salt and pepper on all sides. In a large, deep, heavy frying pan or Dutch oven over medium heat, melt butter. Add chicken pieces, about half at a time, and brown on all sides, removing them as they brown. When all chicken is browned, pour off and discard all fat in pan.

2. Return chicken to pan. Sprinkle with savory, cloves, and lemon rind. Add green onions, vermouth, and broth. Bring to a boil, cover, reduce heat, and simmer until chicken is tender (about 1 hour). Remove chicken to a serving dish and keep warm.

3. Stir cream into liquid in pan and bring to a boil over high heat. Meanwhile, snap off and discard fibrous ends of asparagus spears; cook spears, uncovered, in a small amount of boiling salted water in a wide frying pan (or steam on a rack over boiling water) just until bright green and tender-crisp (8 to 10 minutes). Arrange asparagus around the chicken on serving dish.

4. When cream mixture is reduced by about a third, reduce heat to low. In a small bowl beat egg yolk with lemon juice. Beat in a little of the cream mixture. Then stir egg yolk mixture into cream mixture, stirring constantly, until sauce is slightly thickened. *Do not boil.* Taste, and add salt if necessary. Pour sauce over chicken and asparagus.

Serves 6.

GOLDEN CHICKEN STEW WITH CHEESE DUMPLINGS

Choose an attractive Dutch oven in which to stew this creamy chicken dish. After the fluffy, cheese-flecked dumplings have steamed atop the bubbling chicken, the stew is served directly from the pot.

- *4½ to 5 pounds meaty chicken pieces (thighs, drumsticks, and breasts)*
  Salt, white pepper, ground nutmeg, and paprika
- *2 tablespoons butter or margarine*
- *2 shallots, finely chopped (about ¼ cup)*
- *½ pound large mushrooms, quartered*
- *1 stalk celery, thinly sliced*
- *3 medium carrots, sliced about ⅛ inch thick*
- *½ teaspoon dried tarragon*
- *¼ teaspoon dried thyme*
- *2 cups water*
- *½ cup each dry white wine and whipping cream*
- *3 tablespoons cornstarch, blended with 3 tablespoons cold water*
- *½ cup shelled fresh or frozen peas*
- *¼ cup chopped parsley*

Nippy Cheese Dumplings

- *2 cups flour*
- *1 tablespoon baking powder*
- *½ teaspoon salt*
  Pinch ground nutmeg
- *⅓ cup shredded sharp Cheddar cheese*
- *¼ cup butter or margarine*
- *1 cup milk*

1. Sprinkle chicken pieces lightly on all sides with salt, pepper, nutmeg, and paprika. In a 4½- to 5-quart Dutch oven over medium heat, melt butter. Add chicken pieces, about half at a time, and brown lightly on all sides, removing them as they brown.

2. To same pan add shallots and mushrooms; cook, stirring occasionally, until mushrooms brown lightly. Spoon off and discard as much fat as possible. Mix in celery and carrots. Return chicken pieces to pot. Sprinkle with tarragon and thyme. Add the water and wine. Bring to a boil, cover, reduce heat, and simmer until chicken is tender (1 to 1¼ hours).

3. Meanwhile, prepare Nippy Cheese Dumplings.

4. Remove pot from heat. Remove and reserve chicken pieces. Skim and discard fat from cooking liquid. Blend in cream. Place over medium heat; blend in cornstarch mixture. Cook, stirring, until mixture thickens and boils. Add peas and parsley; then return chicken pieces to sauce. Reduce heat to low.

5. Using 2 tablespoons to shape them, drop rounded dumplings about 1 inch apart over chicken pieces. To prevent the dough from sticking, dip spoons into the sauce before forming the next dumpling. Cover and simmer until dumplings feel firm when touched lightly (15 to 20 minutes; do not uncover until dumplings have cooked for 15 minutes).

6. Serve directly from Dutch oven.

Serves 6 to 8.

Nippy Cheese Dumplings In a large bowl stir together flour, baking powder, salt, nutmeg, and cheese. Using 2 forks or a pastry blender, cut in butter until mixture resembles coarse crumbs. Add milk *all at once,* stirring just until all ingredients are moistened and a soft dough forms.

CHICKEN WITH SHALLOTS

The shallot, a member of the onion family, has a taste that is at the same time more pungent and less strident than that of the onion. Poached and then caramelized, shallots are the crowning touch for chicken quarters cooked in wine and cream.

> 1 chicken (3 to 3½ lbs), cut in quarters
>   Salt and white pepper
> ¼ cup butter or margarine
> 10 shallots
> 1 cup dry white wine
> 1 cup whipping cream
> 1½ tablespoons lemon juice
> 2 teaspoons sugar
> 2 tablespoons water

1. Sprinkle chicken lightly with salt and pepper. In a large, deep frying pan over medium heat, melt 2 tablespoons of the butter. Add chicken and brown well on all sides. When you turn chicken to brown last side, add 2 of the shallots (finely chopped).

2. Add wine, cream, and lemon juice. Bring to a boil, cover, reduce heat, and simmer until chicken is tender (about 40 minutes).

3. Meanwhile, blanch remaining 8 shallots in boiling water for about 1 minute; drain and peel. In a small, heavy pan, combine shallots, the remaining 2 tablespoons butter, and the sugar. Add the water and bring to a boil over high heat, shaking pan and stirring mixture until shallots are coated with an amber caramel sauce. Watch carefully during last stages to prevent sugar mixture from burning or sticking to pan. Remove from heat.

4. Remove chicken quarters to a warm serving plate. Skim and discard fat from cooking liquid if needed. Bring to a boil, stirring, over high heat, and reduce slightly. Blend in shallot mixture, pour sauce over chicken, and serve at once.

Serves 4.

POACHED STUFFED CHICKEN GASCONY

Equating prosperity with "a chicken in every pot" is not a modern idea. It goes back to Henri IV, a sixteenth-century French king. What he had in mind was the *poule au pot* of his native Bearn in southwestern France. This is a contemporary version from neighboring Gascony.

> 1 chicken (3½ to 4 lbs)
> 2 leeks
> 1 medium onion, slivered
> 2 medium carrots, thinly sliced
> 1 medium turnip, peeled, cut in wedges, and thinly sliced
> 1 stalk celery, thinly sliced on the diagonal
> 4 cups Rich Chicken Broth (see page 8) or 2 cans (14½ oz each) chicken broth and ½ cup water
> ½ pound small whole green beans, ends snapped off
>   Coarse salt

Stuffing

> 6 slices French bread (crusts removed)
> ½ cup diced ham
> 1 whole chicken breast (about 1 lb), boned, skinned, and cut in chunks
>   Liver reserved from the chicken
> 2 eggs
> 1 clove garlic, minced or pressed
> 2 tablespoons lightly packed parsley leaves
> ¼ cup whipping cream
> ⅛ teaspoon ground nutmeg
> ½ teaspoon salt
>   Pinch white pepper
> 1 tablespoon Armagnac or brandy

1. Rinse chicken and pat dry; reserve liver for Stuffing and remaining giblets for other uses. Remove and discard any excess fat.

2. Prepare Stuffing and fill cavity of chicken with it; then skewer or sew chicken closed securely. Place the stuffed chicken in a 4½- to 5-quart Dutch oven.

3. Cut off root ends of leeks; remove and discard coarse outer leaves. Cut off and discard green tops. Clean, drain, and slice leeks about ¼ inch thick. Add sliced leeks to Dutch oven with onion, carrots, turnip, celery, and broth. Bring broth to a boil over medium heat; then cover, reduce heat, and simmer until chicken is very tender (about 1½ hours). Remove chicken to a warm, deep platter and keep it warm.

4. To boiling broth add green beans; cook, uncovered, until they are tender-crisp (8 to 10 minutes). Using a slotted spoon, remove vegetables to a serving bowl (or arrange around chicken on platter). Ladle about ½ cup of the broth over vegetables. (Strain remaining broth and freeze it for other uses.)

5. Carve chicken; serve with stuffing on deep, rimmed plates with vegetables and broth spooned over. Accompany with coarse salt.

Serves 4 to 6.

Stuffing Tear bread in pieces and place in food processor, process until fine crumbs form, and transfer to a large bowl. (You should have about 3 cups.) To processor add ham and chicken breast and process until they have the consistency of finely ground meat; add to bread. Then, in processor combine liver, eggs, garlic, parsley, cream, nutmeg, salt, pepper, and Armagnac; process until smooth. Mix lightly but thoroughly into bread-meat mixture.

Note Any stuffing that does not fit into the chicken can be wrapped in blanched cabbage leaves, filling each leaf with about 3 tablespoons of stuffing. Fasten each roll with a wooden pick. Poach in the broth for 15 minutes, adding the rolls 5 to 7 minutes before the green beans.

CHICKEN RAGOÛT

This version of a *navarin* uses chicken instead of lamb. It also offers colorful vegetables complemented by a thin, crisp gratin of potatoes.

- 1 chicken (3 to 3½ lbs), cut up (reserve giblets for other uses)
  Salt, white pepper, and paprika
- 3 tablespoons butter or margarine
- 1 tablespoon salad oil
- 3 shallots, finely chopped (about ⅓ cup)
- ½ pound large mushrooms, quartered
- 2 cloves garlic, minced or pressed
- ½ teaspoon each *dry mustard and dried basil*
- ¼ teaspoon dried rosemary, crumbled
- 8 small white boiling onions
- 1 large tomato, peeled, seeded, and chopped
- 1 package (12 oz) fresh baby carrots, trimmed
- ¾ cup each *dry white wine and Rich Chicken Broth (see page 8) or canned chicken broth*
- ¼ pound edible-pod peas, ends and strings removed
- 1 bunch (about 6) green onions, trimmed to about 6 inches
- 6 baby artichokes, about 2½ inches or less in diameter (directions for preparing follow) or 1 package (9 oz) frozen artichoke hearts, cooked according to package directions

1. Sprinkle chicken pieces with salt, pepper, and paprika. In a large, deep, heavy frying pan or Dutch oven over medium heat, melt 2 tablespoons of butter with the oil. Add chicken pieces, half at a time, and brown well, removing them as they brown.

2. When all chicken is browned, pour off all but about 2 tablespoons of the drippings. To pan add shallots and mushrooms and cook, stirring often,

until mushrooms brown lightly. Mix in garlic, dry mustard, basil, rosemary, and boiling onions; then add tomato and carrots. Return chicken to pan. Pour in wine and broth. Bring to a boil, cover, reduce heat, and cook until chicken and carrots are tender (about 1 hour).

3. During about the last 5 minutes chicken cooks, place edible-pod peas and green onions on top of chicken pieces to steam until they are bright green and tender-crisp.

4. Using a slotted spoon, remove chicken pieces and vegetables to a warm, deep platter, arranging them attractively. Bring cooking liquid to a boil and cook, stirring, until reduced and beginning to thicken. Remove from heat and add remaining 1 tablespoon butter (cut in small pieces) one piece at a time, stirring after each addition. Taste, and add salt if needed. Add artichokes and mix to coat with sauce; then pour sauce over chicken.

Serves 6.

To Prepare Baby Artichokes Cut off and discard top third of each artichoke, peel off outer leaves down to pale green inner ones, peel stem, and cut each artichoke in half lengthwise. As you finish preparing each artichoke, immerse it in a bowl filled with 8 cups cold water to which 2 tablespoons distilled white vinegar have been added. Put prepared artichokes in 6 cups boiling salted water in a 3-quart saucepan; when boiling resumes, cover and boil until artichokes are tender when pierced with a fork (about 15 minutes). Drain well and keep warm until ready to add to sauce.

BRAISED DUCKLING WITH CASSIS

Chicken is not the only fowl that takes well to cooking in enough liquid to qualify as a stew. This quartered duckling in a fruity brown sauce makes a handsome company dish to serve with thin, crisp French fries or a bulgur wheat pilaf, a green vegetable such as Brussels sprouts, and a full-bodied red wine.

If you buy a frozen duckling, you will have to cut it in quarters yourself. First cut off and discard the wing tips (or reserve them to make broth). Then cut along both sides of the backbone and remove it. Next cut through the breastbone and the wishbone—this gives you two halves; cut each crosswise midway between the drumstick and wing. As you work with the duckling, remove and discard all the surface fat that you can. Quartering the duckling before cooking may sound like trouble, but it is far easier than carving it at the table.

- 1 duckling (4½ to 5 lbs), cut in quarters
  Salt, white pepper, and ground nutmeg
- 3 tablespoons butter or margarine
- 1 tablespoon peanut oil
- 2 cloves garlic, minced or pressed
- 2 tablespoons cassis (black currant) or raspberry wine vinegar
- 2 teaspoons tomato paste
- ¼ cup dried currants
- 1 cup Rich Chicken Broth (see page 8) or canned chicken broth
- ⅓ cup each *dry white wine and crème de cassis (black currant liqueur)*
- 1 tablespoon flour

1. Sprinkle quartered duckling on all sides with salt, pepper, and nutmeg. In a large, deep, heavy frying pan over medium heat, melt 2 tablespoons of the butter with the oil. Add duckling and brown well on all sides, removing pieces as they brown.

2. Pour off and discard all but a glazing of the fat in the pan; add garlic, vinegar, and tomato paste, stirring to loosen browned bits from pan. Return duckling to pan. Sprinkle with currants. Add broth, wine, and cassis. Bring to a boil, cover, reduce heat, and simmer until duckling is very tender (about 1 hour).

3. Preheat oven to 400° F. Meanwhile, in a small bowl soften remaining 1 tablespoon butter and mix smoothly with flour. Remove duckling quarters to a deep, ovenproof platter or casserole in a single layer and place, uncovered, in oven while completing sauce.

4. Skim surface fat from cooking liquid and discard. Bring to a boil, stirring, over high heat. Blend in butter-and-flour mixture in bits, stirring until sauce thickens. Taste, and add salt if needed. Pour sauce over duckling and serve at once.

Serves 4.

The flavor of black currant, in the form of cassis vinegar and crème de cassis liqueur, spikes this braised duckling and its gleaming sauce. Because it is difficult to carve, the duckling is cut into quarters before cooking.

TIME-SAVING CHICKEN STEWS

Chicken is economical and cooks quickly, especially when divided into parts. If you buy several whole birds, you can cut them into serving pieces to freeze and use later in recipes that call for whole legs (thighs attached), breasts, or whatever. Freeze packets of bony pieces and bones you have removed from breasts, as well; then you will have them ready when you want to make Rich Chicken Broth (see page 8).

SHERRIED CHICKEN LIVERS WITH POLENTA

Polenta can be made ahead and refrigerated overnight so that you can serve it with a rich, red chicken liver sauce in a jiffy as a weeknight supper.

  3 slices bacon, cut crosswise in ½-inch-wide strips
  1 pound chicken livers, cut in halves
  Salt and pepper
  1 large onion, slivered
  ¼ pound mushrooms, sliced
  1 large clove garlic, minced or pressed
  ½ teaspoon each dried basil and oregano
  ¼ teaspoon dried savory
  1 can (6 oz) tomato paste
  ¾ cup each dry sherry and Rich Chicken Broth (see page 8) or canned chicken broth
  1 tablespoon each butter or margarine and olive oil
  ¼ cup chopped parsley
  Grated Parmesan cheese

Polenta

  2 cups water
  ¼ teaspoon salt
  ⅔ cup polenta
  1 tablespoon butter or margarine
  ¼ cup grated Parmesan cheese

1. Prepare Polenta and refrigerate it.

2. In a large, heavy frying pan over medium heat, cook bacon in its own drippings until browned; remove with a slotted spoon and drain on paper towels. Sprinkle chicken livers lightly with salt and pepper. Cook livers, about half at a time, in bacon drippings until well browned, removing them from pan as they brown.

3. To pan add onion and mushrooms; cook, stirring often, until mushrooms brown lightly. Mix in garlic, basil, oregano, and savory. Then blend in tomato paste, sherry, and broth.

4. Reduce heat to medium-low and boil gently, uncovered, stirring occasionally, until sauce is thick (10 to 12 minutes). Meanwhile, turn loaf of polenta out onto a board and cut in ½-inch-thick slices. In a large, heavy frying pan over medium-high heat, melt butter with oil. Add polenta slices and brown lightly on all sides, turning carefully. Keep hot.

5. When sauce is thick, return chicken livers (and any liquid that accumulated as they stood) to sauce and cook just until they are heated through (2 to 3 minutes). Taste, and add salt if needed. Sprinkle with parsley and bacon.

6. Spoon chicken livers and sauce over hot polenta. Serve with Parmesan cheese to add to taste.

Serves 4.

Polenta In a large, deep saucepan over high heat, bring the water and salt to a rapid boil; using a whisk, gradually stir in polenta. Reduce heat and boil gently, stirring often to prevent sticking and lumping, until mixture is very thick and pulls away from sides of pan when stirred (10 to 15 minutes). Blend in butter and Parmesan cheese. Turn mixture into a well-greased small loaf pan (about 3½ inches by 7½ inches). Cover and refrigerate until firm enough to slice (1 to 2 hours or overnight).

HONEYED CHICKEN WITH APRICOTS

If you enjoy chicken combined with fruit, try this dish during apricot season. It's good with brown rice.

  1 chicken (3 to 3½ lbs), cut in quarters (reserve giblets for other uses)
  Salt and ground allspice
  1 tablespoon each butter or margarine and salad oil
  1 medium onion, thinly slivered
  1 small clove garlic, minced or pressed
  ½ teaspoon each ground turmeric and ground ginger
  ¼ teaspoon ground coriander
  1 cinnamon stick (2 to 3 inches)
  ½ cup water
  ¼ cup honey
  1 lemon, thinly sliced, with seeds removed
  4 apricots, pitted and cut in quarters

1. Sprinkle chicken lightly on all sides with salt and allspice. In a large, deep frying pan over medium heat, melt butter with oil. Add chicken and brown well on all sides.

2. When chicken pieces are nearly browned on last sides, spoon off and discard all but a scant 2 tablespoons of the drippings (if necessary). Then add onion and garlic around chicken. Sprinkle with turmeric, ginger, and coriander. Add cinnamon stick in among chicken quarters.

3. Add the water and honey. Arrange lemon slices in a single layer over chicken. Bring to a boil, cover, reduce heat, and simmer until chicken is tender (45 to 50 minutes).

4. Remove chicken and lemons to a warm, deep serving platter and keep warm. Bring liquid to a boil over high heat, stirring to blend in brown drippings from pan, and reduce until syrupy. Add apricots, turning them in the sauce just long enough to glaze and heat through.

5. Spoon sauce and apricots over chicken on the serving platter.

Serves 4.

CREAMY STUFFED CHICKEN BREASTS WITH LEEKS

Although they look like a company dish, these rolled chicken breasts are easy enough to cook after a hard day's work—especially if you've thought ahead and pounded and stuffed the chicken the night before.

> 3 leeks
> 2 whole chicken breasts (4 halves, about 2 lbs in all), halved, boned, and skinned White pepper, nutmeg, and paprika
> 3 tablespoons chopped parsley
> 4 thin slices baked ham
> 1 tablespoon each butter or margarine and salad oil
> 1 clove garlic, minced or pressed
> ½ cup Rich Chicken Broth (see page 8) or canned chicken broth
> ½ cup whipping cream
> 1 tablespoon lemon juice Salt (optional)

1. Cut off root ends of leeks; remove and discard coarse outer leaves. Cut off and discard green tops so that leeks are about 8 inches long. Split lengthwise, from leafy end, cutting to within about 1 inch of root end. Soak in cold water for several minutes; then separate leaves under running water to rinse away any clinging grit; drain. Slice about ¼ inch thick.

2. Lightly sprinkle chicken breasts on all sides with pepper, nutmeg, and paprika. Place, one at a time, between sheets of plastic wrap and pound with flat side of a mallet until each breast is about ⅛ inch thick.

3. Place pounded chicken breasts, boned sides up, side by side. Sprinkle 1 tablespoon of the parsley evenly over the 4 breasts. Then place a slice of ham over each. (Trim edges of ham, if necessary, so that they do not extend beyond the chicken.) Fold sides in, then roll up each breast from one end to make about 3½-inch-wide rolls. Fasten ends with small skewers or wooden toothpicks.

4. In a 10-inch frying pan over medium heat, melt butter with oil. Add chicken breast rolls and brown quickly on all sides. Mix leeks, garlic, and remaining 2 tablespoons parsley around chicken. Add broth, bring to a boil, cover, reduce heat, and simmer until chicken is cooked through (20 to 25 minutes).

5. Transfer chicken rolls to a warm serving dish and keep warm. To pan add cream. Cook over high heat, stirring often, until large, shiny bubbles form and liquid is slightly thickened. Mix in lemon juice. Taste, and add salt if needed.

6. Spoon sauce over chicken and serve at once.

Serves 4.

CHICKEN LEGS WITH PIPERADE

Piperade is a savory vegetable mélange from southwest France. It's usually served with eggs, but here it makes a wonderful sauce and side dish in one for chicken. Add rice to complete the main course.

> 4 whole chicken legs (thighs attached; about 3 lbs in all) Salt, pepper, and ground cloves
> 1 orange
> 2 tablespoons olive oil
> 1 medium onion, thinly slivered
> 1 each red and green bell pepper, seeded and cut in strips
> 2 cloves garlic, minced or pressed
> ¼ teaspoon ground turmeric
> ½ teaspoon dried basil
> 1 can (1 lb) tomatoes
> ¼ cup chopped parsley
> 1 teaspoon cornstarch, blended with 2 teaspoons water

1. Lightly sprinkle chicken legs on all sides with salt, pepper, and cloves. Grate rind and squeeze juice from orange; reserve both.

2. In a large, deep, heavy frying pan, heat oil over medium heat. Add chicken legs and brown well on all sides, removing them as they brown. Pour off and discard all but about 2 tablespoons of the drippings.

3. To same pan add onion and bell pepper strips. Cook, stirring, until onion is soft but not browned. Mix in garlic, turmeric, and basil. Return chicken to pan. Add tomatoes (coarsely chopped) and their liquid, reserved orange juice, half the grated orange rind, and half the parsley.

4. Bring to a boil, cover, reduce heat, and simmer until chicken is tender (about 45 minutes). Remove chicken to a warm serving dish and keep warm. If necessary, skim and discard fat from cooking liquid. Bring to a boil over high heat and cook, stirring, until liquid is reduced by about a third. Blend in cornstarch mixture, stirring until sauce is thickened and clear. Taste, and add salt if needed.

5. Spoon sauce over chicken. Serve sprinkled with remaining orange rind and chopped parsley.

Serves 4.

115

BASIL CELEBRATION

Fresh Mushroom Salad

*Chicken With Basil
and Walnuts*

*Garlic-Sautéed
Crookneck Squash*

Crusty Rolls

Butter

*Mrs. Winbigler's
Chocolate Pie*

Light Red Wine

Coffee

When fresh basil is in season in your garden or local store, serve guests this dinner. Start with mushrooms in a mustardy vinaigrette, followed by chicken topped with a basil sauce and accompanied with sautéed squash. For a final caress, savor a chocolate meringue pie.

FRESH MUSHROOM SALAD

1 *pound mushrooms, thinly
sliced*
Butter lettuce leaves
Chopped parsley, for garnish

Red Wine Vinaigrette Dressing

2 *tablespoons red wine vinegar*
½ *teaspoon salt*
1 *teaspoon Dijon mustard*
⅛ *teaspoon white pepper*
1 *shallot, finely chopped
(about 2 tbsp)*
1 *tablespoon chopped parsley*
¼ *cup salad oil*
2 *tablespoons olive oil*

1. Prepare Red Wine Vinaigrette dressing; shortly before serving, blend again until dressing is well combined.

2. In a shallow serving bowl or on individual salad plates, arrange mushrooms on lettuce leaves. Pour dressing over mushrooms.

3. Sprinkle with parsley to serve.

Serves 4.

Red Wine Vinaigrette Dressing
In a medium bowl blend vinegar, salt, mustard, pepper, shallot, and parsley. Beating with a fork or whisk, gradually blend in salad and olive oils until dressing is well combined.

CHICKEN WITH BASIL AND WALNUTS

2 *tablespoons olive oil*
½ *cup coarsely chopped walnuts*
1 *chicken (3 to 3½ lbs), cut up
(save giblets for other uses)*
Salt and pepper
2 *large cloves garlic, minced
or pressed*
½ *cup chopped parsley*
1 *cup lightly packed fresh
basil leaves*
⅓ *cup dry white wine*
1 *tablespoon lemon juice*
¾ *cup whipping cream*
Grated Parmesan cheese

1. In a large, deep, heavy frying pan, heat oil over medium heat. Add walnuts and stir until lightly browned. Remove from pan and reserve.

2. Sprinkle chicken with salt and pepper on all sides. Brown in same pan, ending with skin sides up. Discard most of the drippings. Add garlic; half *each* of the parsley and basil; and wine, lemon juice, and cream.

3. Bring to a boil, cover, reduce heat, and simmer until chicken is tender (40 to 45 minutes). Remove chicken to a serving dish and keep warm.

4. Bring cooking liquid to a boil over high heat. Add remaining parsley and basil and half of the walnuts. Transfer to blender and whirl until smooth. Return to pan, add salt if needed, and reheat. Pour over chicken. Sprinkle with remaining walnuts.

5. Serve with cheese to sprinkle over each serving to taste.

Serves 4 to 6.

MRS. WINBIGLER'S CHOCOLATE PIE

2¼ *cups sugar*
¼ *cup flour*
¼ *cup unsweetened cocoa*
Pinch salt
4 *eggs, separated*
2 *cups milk*
2 *tablespoons butter or
margarine*
1 *tablespoon vanilla extract*
Pinch cream of tartar

Chocolate Press-In Pastry

1 *cup flour*
2 *teaspoons unsweetened cocoa*
3 *tablespoons sugar*
⅓ *cup cold butter or margarine*
1 *egg yolk*
¼ *teaspoon vanilla extract*

1. Preheat oven to 450° F. Press Chocolate Press-In Pastry into bottom and up sides of a 9-inch pie pan. Bake until lightly brown and firm to the touch (8 to 10 minutes). Let pastry cool in pan on a wire rack. Reduce oven temperature to 350° F.

2. In a heavy 2- to 2½-quart saucepan, stir together 2 cups of the sugar, flour, cocoa, and salt until well combined. Add egg yolks. Then, using a whisk, gradually blend in milk. Add butter. Place over direct medium-low heat and cook, *stirring constantly,* until mixture boils and thickens.

3. Remove filling from heat and blend in vanilla. Let cool slightly (15 to 20 minutes). Spread in pastry.

4. In a large bowl beat the 4 egg whites until frothy; blend in cream of tartar and continue beating until soft peaks form. Gradually add the remaining ¼ cup sugar, beating until mixture is stiff and glossy. Spread meringue lightly over chocolate filling. Bake until the meringue is a pale golden brown (8 to 10 minutes).

Serves 6 to 8.

Chocolate Press-In Pastry In a medium bowl mix flour, cocoa, and sugar until there are no lumps of cocoa. Cut in butter until mixture resembles coarse crumbs. Beat egg yolk with vanilla. With a fork stir egg mixture lightly into flour mixture; then use your hands to press dough into a smooth, flattened ball.

Celebrate the summer harvest of fresh basil with this chicken dish. Walnuts add substance to basil sauce, which is whirled smooth in the blender.

CHICKEN ROSEMARY WITH SHERRY

Cook this chicken in either a large range-top frying pan or an electric one. The idea is to cook at a temperature that eventually will reduce most of the liquid to a caramel-like glaze for the chicken pieces. If you like, you can cook tiny red potatoes among the chicken pieces; add them just before you cover the pan.

> 1 chicken (3 to 3½ lbs),
>   cut up (reserve giblets
>   for other uses)
>   Salt and pepper
> 2 tablespoons olive oil
> 1 large shallot, finely chopped
>   (about 2 tbsp)
> 2 large cloves garlic, minced
>   or pressed
> 3 sprigs fresh rosemary or
>   1½ teaspoons dried rosemary,
>   crumbled
> ¼ cup dry sherry
> 2 tablespoons lemon juice
>   Chopped parsley, for garnish

1. Sprinkle chicken pieces on all sides with salt and pepper.

2. In a large, deep, heavy frying pan or electric frying pan, heat oil over medium heat. Mix in shallot and garlic. Add chicken, skin sides down, to coat with oil mixture. Turn to brown undersides of pieces; then turn and brown skin sides slightly. Without turning chicken again, add rosemary sprigs or sprinkle with rosemary. Pour in sherry.

3. Cover, reduce heat to medium-low, and cook until chicken is tender (40 to 45 minutes). During last 5 minutes, uncover frying pan or open vent of electric frying pan to reduce most of the remaining cooking liquid.

4. Arrange chicken pieces skin sides up on a warm platter. Pour off and discard fat in pan. Add lemon juice, stirring over medium-low heat to blend in caramelized bits. Spoon over chicken. Sprinkle with parsley.

Serves 4 to 6.

LEMON CHICKEN BREASTS

If you are adept with a wok, it is a perfect utensil to use when you cook this speedy interpretation of a favorite Chinese way with chicken breasts.

> 3 chicken breasts (6 halves,
>   2½ to 3 lbs in all), boned
>   and skinned
> 2 lemons
> 1 tablespoon each butter or
>   margarine and salad oil
> 1 clove garlic, minced or pressed
> ⅓ cup Rich Chicken Broth
>   (see page 8) or canned
>   chicken broth
> 2 teaspoons each cornstarch
>   and sugar
> 1 tablespoon each soy sauce
>   and water
>   Salt (optional)

1. Cut chicken breasts crosswise in ½-inch-wide strips. Grate rind from 1 lemon and squeeze juice; reserve both. Cut other lemon in half, squeeze juice from 1 of the halves, and add to reserved juices. Slice remaining half lemon thinly and reserve the slices for garnish.

2. In a large, heavy frying pan, electric frying pan, or wok over medium-high heat, melt butter with oil. Add chicken breast strips, about half at a time, and brown on all sides, removing them as they brown. When all chicken is browned, return it to pan and mix in garlic.

3. Add chicken broth and reserved lemon juice. Bring to a boil, cover, reduce heat, and simmer until chicken is just firm and opaque (5 to 6 minutes; do not overcook). Meanwhile, in a small bowl blend cornstarch smoothly with sugar, soy sauce, and the water.

4. Add lemon rind and soy sauce mixture to chicken, bring to a boil over medium-high heat, and stir until thickened and smooth. Taste, and add salt if needed.

5. Garnish with lemon slices.

Serves 4 to 6.

TURKEY BREAST WITH MUSHROOMS AND GARLIC

This quick-cooking main dish will remind you of scaloppine, but it's made with reasonably priced turkey breast. That's no reason not to serve it with traditional Italian accompaniments such as buttered tagliarini and steamed chard or spinach.

> 1 to 1¼ pounds boneless
>   turkey breast, sliced
>   about ¼ inch thick
>   Salt, white pepper, and
>   ground nutmeg
> 2 tablespoons each butter or
>   margarine and olive oil
> ½ pound mushrooms, sliced
> 2 shallots, finely chopped
>   (about ¼ cup)
> 2 cloves garlic, minced or
>   pressed
> ¼ teaspoon dried sage
> 3 tablespoons chopped parsley
> ⅓ cup dry white wine
> 2 tablespoons lemon juice

1. Cut turkey breast slices crosswise in about ½-inch-wide strips. Sprinkle lightly on all sides with salt, pepper, and nutmeg.

2. In a large, heavy frying pan over medium-high heat, melt butter with oil. Add turkey breast strips, about a third at a time, and brown them well on all sides, removing them when they are brown.

3. To pan add mushrooms and shallots and cook, stirring, until mushrooms brown lightly and most of their liquid has cooked away. Mix in garlic. Sprinkle with sage and 2 tablespoons of the parsley. Add wine.

4. Bring to a boil over high heat and cook, stirring, until liquid is reduced and syrupy. Blend in lemon juice; then return turkey strips to pan. Stir to heat through and to coat them with mushroom sauce.

5. Sprinkle with remaining parsley and serve at once.

Serves 4.

FISH AND SHELLFISH STEWS

While fish and seafood are not as easy on the budget as poultry, the tariff is not quite as steep as the price tag might indicate. Consider that fish fillets contain no waste at all—neither fat nor bones—so you can count on more servings per pound than from bone-in poultry. By keeping an eye out for specials, it is often possible to find some truly good buys.

The recipes that follow have been chosen to represent the stew genre because they are all so substantial that there can be no question about their status as main dishes—and rather elegant ones, at that.

BOUILLABAISSE

This interpretation of the classic French seafood mélange comes from the area around Marseilles. It's a fine kettle of fish steaks and fillets, arrayed on a deep platter after cooking. Diners help themselves to a choice of fish, placing it into a pool of the saffron-scented broth in which all were cooked. A hot pepper mayonnaise, or *rouille*, seasons the fish. Toasted croutons of French bread are also offered.

Complete the menu with a green salad that includes marinated artichoke hearts and tiny black Niçoise olives, and a white Zinfandel or light red wine. Add a tart citrus dessert, such as chilled lemon mousse.

> ¼ cup olive oil
> 1 clove garlic, thinly slivered
> 1½ pounds lingcod steaks
> 1 can (8 oz) tomato sauce
> 1 teaspoon grated orange rind
> ⅛ teaspoon fennel seed, crushed
> ⅛ teaspoon powdered saffron or ¼ teaspoon saffron threads
> 4 cups Fish Broth (see page 11)
> 1½ pounds sea bass steaks
> 1 halibut steak (¾ to 1 lb)
> 1 pound red snapper fillets
> Salt (optional)
> Baguette Croutons (prepare a triple recipe; see page 17)

Hot Pepper Mayonnaise

> ⅓ cup each *salad oil and olive oil*
> 3 large cloves garlic, minced or pressed
> 2 tablespoons lemon juice
> ½ teaspoon salt
> ¼ teaspoon cayenne pepper
> 2 egg yolks

1. In a 5½- to 6-quart kettle or Dutch oven, heat olive oil over medium heat. Stir in garlic. Add lingcod and brown lightly on all sides, turning carefully. Add tomato sauce, orange rind, fennel seed, and saffron; pour in Fish Broth.

2. Bring slowly to a boil, reduce heat, cover, and simmer for 30 minutes.

3. Add sea bass steaks and halibut. Increase heat to medium-low, cover, and cook without disturbing for 5 minutes. Add red snapper fillets, cover again, and continue cooking until snapper flakes easily when tested with a fork (8 to 10 minutes).

4. While snapper cooks, prepare Hot Pepper Mayonnaise.

5. Carefully remove fish from broth with a slotted spatula and arrange on a deep, warm platter. Taste broth, and add salt if needed. Ladle broth into large, shallow soup bowls and pass fish at the table for guests to take as much as they wish. Accompany with Hot Pepper Mayonnaise for seasoning and Baguette Croutons to sprinkle on top of the fish.

Serves 8 to 10.

Hot Pepper Mayonnaise In measuring cup mix salad oil and olive oil. In blender combine garlic, lemon juice, salt, cayenne, and egg yolks. Cover and turn on blender. *Immediately* begin pouring in oils in a very slow, steady stream. Whirl until all the oil is added and mayonnaise is thick and smooth.

Makes about 1 cup.

HOMEMADE TOMATO SAUCE

Pick or purchase vine-ripened tomatoes during the summer and make batches of sweet and tasty tomato sauce to use in your stews. Freeze it for year-round use.

1. *Peel the tomatoes. The simplest way to do this is to drop tomatoes into boiling water for about 30 seconds, then, using a slotted spoon, lift them out and immediately plunge them into cold water. The skin will peel off easily.*

2. *Cut tomatoes in half and squeeze each half gently to remove watery liquid and seeds. Discard everything except the actual tomato shell.*

3. *In a blender or food processor, whirl tomato shells. Combine purée with sautéed onions, garlic, olive oil, a pinch of sugar, basil, and salt and pepper to taste.*

4. *Cook over medium-high heat stirring frequently until liquid is reduced and the sauce thickens.*

5. *Cool sauce and spoon into freezer containers, leaving headroom for expansion. Freeze up to 4 months.*

EASY SEAFOOD SUPPER

Olives

Bread Sticks

Fish Stew With Sherry

Rice With Peas

Fresh Peach Crisp

White Jug Wine

Coffee

Olives and bread sticks are simple and good appetizers. Enjoy them with a glass of dry sherry before this meal.

It all goes together quickly, because the fish stew needs very little cooking. While the sauce cooks, put together the peach dessert to bake during the main course. Serve the stew over steamed rice to which you have added shelled fresh or frozen peas during the last five minutes of cooking.

FISH STEW WITH SHERRY

2 *tablespoons* each *butter or margarine and olive oil*

1 *large onion, finely chopped*

1 *green bell pepper, seeded and chopped*

1 *medium carrot, shredded*

1 *teaspoon paprika*

½ *teaspoon* each *salt and dried basil*

¼ *teaspoon ground turmeric*

2 *cloves garlic, minced or pressed*

2 *tablespoons tomato paste*

3 *medium tomatoes, peeled and chopped*

1 *cup Fish Broth (see page 11) or Rich Chicken Broth (see page 8) or canned chicken broth*

½ *cup dry sherry*

1 *to 1¼ pounds firm, mild-flavored fish fillets, cut in 1-inch squares*

¼ *pound tiny peeled cooked shrimp (optional)*

2 *tablespoons chopped parsley Lemon wedges, for garnish*

1. In a large, deep frying pan or 3½- to 4-quart Dutch oven over medium heat, melt butter with oil. Add onion, bell pepper, and carrot; cook, stirring often, until onion begins to brown. Mix in paprika, salt, basil, turmeric, garlic, tomato paste, tomatoes, broth, and sherry.

2. Bring to a boil; then boil gently, uncovered, until thick (15 to 20 minutes). Mix in fish and shrimp (if used). Continue cooking until fish is opaque and flakes when tested with a fork (3 to 5 minutes).

3. Mix in parsley. Taste, and add salt if needed. Serve at once accompanied with lemon wedges on the side.

Serves 4.

FRESH PEACH CRISP

4 *large peaches (1½ to 2 lbs)*

½ *cup granulated sugar*

2 *teaspoons quick-cooking tapioca*

½ *teaspoon ground cinnamon*

⅛ *teaspoon ground nutmeg*

½ *cup flour*

½ *cup firmly packed brown sugar*

¼ *cup cold butter or margarine*

½ *cup slivered almonds Ice cream or whipping cream (optional)*

1. Preheat oven to 350° F. To peel peaches, dip, one at a time, in boiling water to cover for 30 seconds each. Plunge into, or rinse with, cold water. Remove from water; then slip off skins with a small knife. Slice peaches thinly. (You should have approximately 3½ to 4 cups.)

2. In a large bowl mix granulated sugar, tapioca, cinnamon, and nutmeg. Add peaches and mix lightly. Let peach mixture stand while preparing topping.

3. For topping, in a medium bowl blend flour and brown sugar. Cut in butter until mixture resembles coarse crumbs. Mix in almonds.

4. Spread peach mixture in a greased shallow 2- to 2½-quart casserole. Cover evenly with topping.

5. Bake, uncovered, until peaches are tender and bubbling and topping is well browned (40 to 45 minutes).

6. Serve either warm or at room temperature with a scoop of ice cream or poured cream, if you wish.

Serves 4 to 6.

The three-funneled ship berthed beside an almond-crusted Fresh Peach Crisp is actually a tureen containing the quick and tasty Fish Stew With Sherry.

TOMATO AND OYSTER STEW

All it takes is one jar of oysters, but with the addition of pasta shells this stew makes three or four servings. Add crusty bread and a big green salad, then sherbet for dessert.

> 3 slices bacon, cut crosswise in ½-inch-wide strips
> 1 large onion, finely chopped
> 2 stalks celery, thinly sliced
> 2 cloves garlic, minced or pressed
> 1 jar (10 fl oz) oysters
> 1 can (8 oz) tomato sauce
> ½ cup dry white wine
> 1 cup Fish Broth (see page 11) or Rich Chicken Broth (see page 8) or canned chicken broth
> ⅛ teaspoon each white pepper and dried marjoram
> ¼ cup chopped parsley
> ⅓ cup small shell-shaped pasta
> Salt (optional)
> Grated Parmesan cheese

1. In a large, deep frying pan over medium heat, cook bacon in its own drippings, stirring often, until browned. Drain on paper towels. Pour off and discard all but 2 tablespoons of the drippings.

2. To pan add onion and celery; cook, stirring often, until soft but not browned. Mix in garlic. Drain oysters, reserving liquid. To onion mixture add oyster liquid, tomato sauce, wine, broth, pepper, marjoram, and half of the parsley. Bring to a boil, add pasta, cover, reduce heat, and boil gently until pasta is just tender (12 to 15 minutes).

3. Mix in bacon and oysters. Cook, uncovered, just until oysters are firm and edges ruffle (2 to 3 minutes). Taste, and add salt if needed. Mix in remaining parsley.

4. Serve stew in shallow bowls with Parmesan cheese to add to taste.

Serves 3 or 4.

POACHED FISH IN AVGOLEMONO

The Greek approach to poached fish involves cooking it with potatoes and then bathing both in a tart lemon sauce, or avgolemono.

> 2 tablespoons olive oil
> 1 medium onion, chopped
> 6 medium-sized new potatoes (about 2 lbs), peeled or unpeeled
> 1 bay leaf
> 3 sprigs parsley
> ¼ teaspoon black peppercorns
> 4 cups Fish Broth (see page 11) or Rich Chicken Broth (see page 8) or canned chicken broth
> 3 large sea bass or other lean, white, firm-flesh fish steaks, ¾ to 1 inch thick (2½ to 3 lbs)
> 3 tablespoons lemon juice
> 2 eggs
> Salt (optional)
> Parsley sprigs and lemon wedges, for garnish

1. In a 4½- to 5-quart kettle, heat olive oil over medium heat. Add onion and cook until soft but not browned. Add potatoes, bay leaf, the 3 sprigs parsley, peppercorns, and broth. Bring to a boil, cover, reduce heat, and boil gently for 30 minutes.

2. Add sea bass steaks on top of potatoes. As soon as liquid begins to boil again, cover, and reduce heat; simmer until potatoes are tender, and fish is opaque and separates into flakes when tested with a fork (10 to 12 minutes).

3. With a slotted spoon transfer fish steaks and potatoes to a warm, large, deep platter; cover lightly with foil and keep warm. Strain broth and measure 1 cup. (Freeze remainder and use as Fish Broth.)

4. In a medium bowl beat lemon juice with eggs until well combined. Return the 1 cup broth to kettle in which fish cooked. Off heat, whisk in egg mixture. Continue whisking over low heat until sauce is just thick enough to coat a metal spoon. *Do not boil.* Taste; add salt if needed.

5. Spoon or pour off any liquid that has accumulated in platter and discard; pour sauce over fish. Garnish with parsley and lemon and serve at once. Cut each fish steak in half and serve in broad, shallow bowls.

Serves 6.

FISHERMAN'S WHARF CIOPPINO

This is a gloriously sloppy dish to eat. With the pieces of cracked crab in their shells, there's nothing to do but wade in with both hands—with lots of paper napkins at the ready. Provide shellfish or nut crackers in case the crab needs more cracking.

Accompany cioppino with hot garlic French bread (preferably sourdough) and a good Chianti. The best dessert is fresh fruit and perhaps some crisp cookies.

> ¼ cup olive oil
> 1 large onion, finely chopped
> 1 red or green bell pepper, seeded and chopped
> 3 cloves garlic, minced or pressed
> ½ cup finely chopped parsley
> 1 teaspoon dried basil
> ½ teaspoon dried oregano
> 1 large can (28 oz) Italian plum tomatoes
> 1 can (6 oz) tomato paste
> 2 cups dry white wine
> 1 teaspoon salt
> ¼ teaspoon coarsely ground pepper
> ¾ to 1 pound rock cod fillets, cut in 1-inch squares
> 2 medium Dungeness crabs (about 1½ lbs each), cooked, cleaned, and cracked
> 1 pound shrimp, shelled and deveined
> 12 fresh clams in shells, scrubbed

1. In a deep, heavy 5½- to 6-quart kettle or Dutch oven, heat olive oil over medium heat. Add onion and bell pepper. Cook, stirring often, until onion is soft but not browned. Mix in garlic, parsley, basil, and oregano. Stir in tomatoes (coarsely chopped) and their liquid, tomato paste, wine, salt, and pepper.

2. Bring to a boil, cover, reduce heat, and simmer for 1 hour. Uncover and boil gently, stirring occasionally, over medium-low heat until sauce is fairly thick (30 to 35 minutes).

3. Add, in order given, rock cod, crabs, shrimp, and clams. Cover and cook until crab meat is heated through, the shrimp are pink, and the clams are open (20 to 25 minutes). Discard any clams that do not open. Taste; add salt if needed.

4. Serve in large, shallow bowls that have been warmed.

Serves 6.

Rock cod fillets, Dungeness crab, shrimp, and clams—food to make a fish lover's mouth water. Use the clam shells as spoons and the tips of the crab claws as picks in order to enjoy every morsel of this Fisherman's Wharf Cioppino.

ELEGANT FISH DINNER

Asparagus or Broccoli
Vinaigrette

Creamy Fish Stew

Fluffy Rice

French Bread

Sweet Butter

Almond Tarts

White Wine

Coffee

A variety of seafood is the centerpiece of this menu. Both the first course, a vegetable vinaigrette, and the dessert tarts can be prepared in advance.

A white wine such as a California Chardonnay would be a lovely choice to accompany the fish, but you might also enjoy a crisp, blushing white Zinfandel or Blanc de Pinot Noir.

CREAMY FISH STEW

> 1 quart (about 1½ lbs)
>   uncooked mussels in shells
> 2 sprigs parsley
> ⅛ teaspoon white peppercorns
> 1½ cups dry white wine
> 3 leeks
> ¼ cup butter
> 3 shallots, finely chopped
> 1 stalk celery, finely chopped
> ½ pound salmon fillet
> 1 pound sole fillets
> 1 pound snapper fillets,
>   cut crosswise into
>   1-inch-wide strips
> ½ pound shrimp, shelled
>   and deveined
> ½ cup whipping cream
> 2 egg yolks
>   Salt (optional)
>   Chopped parsley and lemon
>   wedges, for garnish

1. Discard any mussels that may have opened. Clean mussels by scraping off any barnacles. Then scrub thoroughly with a stiff brush under running water, making sure you get the shells completely clean. Drain mussels.

2. In a 4- to 5-quart kettle, combine mussels, parsley, peppercorns, and wine. Bring to a boil over medium heat, cover, reduce heat, and simmer until mussels have opened (6 to 8 minutes). Discard any mussels that remain closed.

3. Remove mussels from liquid, reserving liquid. Reserve a few mussels in shells for garnish. Remove remaining mussels from shells. (You should have about 1 cup cooked mussels.) Pinch out and discard the "beard" from any mussel that has one.

4. Set mussels aside. Strain the mussel cooking liquid through a dampened cloth and reserve the liquid.

5. Cut off root ends of leeks; remove and discard coarse outer leaves. Cut off and discard green tops. Split lengthwise, from leafy end, cutting to within about 1 inch of root end. Soak in cold water for several minutes; then separate leaves under running water to rinse away any clinging grit; drain. Slice about ¼ inch thick.

6. In a 3½- to 4-quart Dutch oven over medium heat, melt butter. Add leeks, shallots, and celery; cook, stirring often, until vegetables are soft but not browned.

7. Meanwhile, cut salmon fillet in 6 equal pieces. Roll each sole fillet around a piece of salmon. Place rolled sole fillets (with ends on underside to hold rolls together) over vegetables. Add snapper strips and shrimp. Measure out 1½ cups of the strained mussel cooking liquid. Pour this over the fish.

8. When liquid begins to boil, cover, reduce heat, and simmer until fish is opaque and shrimp are pink (8 to 10 minutes). With a slotted spoon transfer sole rolls, snapper strips, and shrimp to a shallow 2-quart casserole; cover them lightly with foil and keep them warm.

9. Add cream to cooking liquid and vegetables. Bring to a boil over high heat and cook, stirring often, until large, shiny bubbles form and liquid is reduced by about half. Remove from heat. In a medium bowl beat egg yolks; beat in a little of the hot liquid. Blend egg yolk mixture into cream mixture. Add mussels. Stir over low heat until sauce is just thickened. *Do not boil.* If liquid has accumulated in the serving dish with the fish, spoon it off and blend it into the sauce. Taste, and add salt if needed. Pour the sauce over the fish.

10. Garnish with chopped parsley and lemon wedges and serve at once.

Serves 6.

ALMOND TARTS

  2 eggs
  1 cup granulated sugar
  ½ cup firmly packed light
    brown sugar
  ¼ teaspoon salt
  2 tablespoons butter or
    margarine, melted
  ½ teaspoon each *vanilla and
    almond extracts*
  1 cup ground almonds
  ¼ cup sliced almonds
  ¼ cup apricot preserves

Cream Cheese Pastry

  ½ cup butter (softened)
  1 small package (3 oz) cream
    cheese (softened)
  1 tablespoon amaretto liqueur
    or brandy
  1¼ cups flour

1. Preheat oven to 350° F. Prepare Cream Cheese Pastry and divide into 10 equal portions; press each into bottom and up sides of a 3½-inch tart pan about 1 inch deep.

2. In a large bowl beat eggs until thick and light colored. Gradually blend in white and brown sugars; then blend in salt, melted butter, and vanilla and almond extracts. Mix in ground almonds.

3. Divide filling evenly among the 10 pastry-lined tart pans; sprinkle each with a heaping teaspoon of the sliced almonds.

4. Bake until pastry and filling are well browned (25 to 30 minutes). Remove pans to a rack to cool for about 10 minutes. Then carefully slip tarts out of pans and onto the rack.

5. In a small pan, stirring often, heat preserves until bubbly. Strain to remove bits of fruit. Brush tops of warm tarts with warm apricot glaze.

Makes 10 tarts.

Cream Cheese Pastry In a medium bowl of electric mixer, cream butter and cream cheese until light and fluffy. Blend in liqueur . Gradually add flour, blending until mixture is smooth.

This fish stew requires last-minute attention, but much of the preparation can be done ahead so that the ingredients are ready to use: Cook the mussels and reserve the liquid; clean the shrimp; prepare the leeks, shallots, and celery; and assemble the salmon-filled sole rolls.

INDEX

U.S. MEASURE AND METRIC MEASURE CONVERSION CHART

		Formulas for Exact Measures			**Rounded Measures for Quick Reference**		
	Symbol	**When you know:**	**Multiply by**	**To find:**			
Mass (Weight)	oz	ounces	28.35	grams	1 oz		= 30 g
	lb	pounds	0.45	kilograms	4 oz		= 115 g
	g	grams	0.035	ounces	8 oz		= 225 g
	kg	kilograms	2.2	pounds	16 oz	= 1 lb	= 450 g
					32 oz	= 2 lb	= 900 g
					36 oz	= 2¼ lb	= 1,000 g (1 kg)
Volume	tsp	teaspoons	5.0	milliliters	¼ tsp	= 1/24 oz	= 1 ml
	tbsp	tablespoons	15.0	milliliters	½ tsp	= 1/12 oz	= 2 ml
	fl oz	fluid ounces	29.57	milliliters	1 tsp	= 1/6 oz	= 5 ml
	c	cups	0.24	liters	1 tbsp	= ½ oz	= 15 ml
	pt	pints	0.47	liters	1 c	= 8 oz	= 250 ml
	qt	quarts	0.95	liters	2 c (1 pt)	= 16 oz	= 500 ml
	gal	gallons	3.785	liters	4 c (1 qt)	= 32 oz	= 1 l.
	ml	milliliters	0.034	fluid ounces	4 qt (1 gal)	= 128 oz	= 3¾ l.
Length	in.	inches	2.54	centimeters	⅜ in.	= 1 cm	
	ft	feet	30.48	centimeters	1 in.	= 2.5 cm	
	yd	yards	0.9144	meters	2 in.	= 5 cm	
	mi	miles	1.609	kilometers	2½ in.	= 6.5 cm	
	km	kilometers	0.621	miles	12 in. (1 ft)	= 30 cm	
	m	meters	1.094	yards	1 yd	= 90 cm	
	cm	centimeters	0.39	inches	100 ft	= 30 m	
					1 mi	= 1.6 km	
Temperature	° F	Fahrenheit	5/9 (after subtracting 32)	Celsius	32° F	= 0° C	
					68 °F	= 20° C	
	° C	Celsius	9/5 (then add 32)	Fahrenheit	212° F	= 100° C	
Area	in.^{2}	square inches	6.452	square centimeters	1 in.^{2}	= 6.5 cm^2	
	ft^2	square feet	929.0	square centimeters	1 ft^2	= 930 cm^2	
	yd^2	square yards	8,361.0	square centimeters	1 yd^2	= 8,360 cm^2	
	a	acres	0.4047	hectares	1 a	= 4,050 m^2	